Crocheting
Easy Blankets, Throws & Wraps

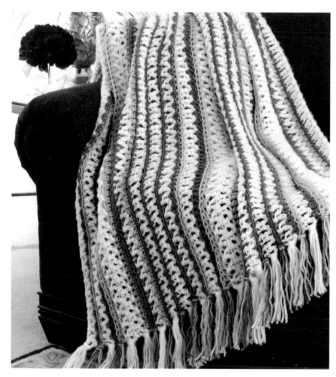

From-Elegant-to-Casual Capelet, page 66

www.companyscoming.com
visit our website

Front Cover: Bold Blocks Afghan, page 38

Crocheting

Copyright © Company's Coming Publishing Limited

First Printing December 2008

Library and Archives Canada Cataloguing in Publication
Crocheting : easy blankets, throws & wraps.
(Creative series)
Includes index.
At head of title: Company's Coming crafts.
ISBN 978-1-897477-01-4
1. Crocheting. 2. Crocheting--Patterns.
I. Series: Creative series (Edmonton, Alta.)
TT820.C94 2008   746.43'4041   C2008-903104-0

Published by
Company's Coming Publishing Limited
2311-96 Street
Edmonton, Alberta, Canada T6N 1G3
Tel: 780-450-6223 Fax: 780-450-1857
www.companyscoming.com

Company's Coming is a registered trademark owned by Company's Coming Publishing Limited

Printed in China

THE COMPANY'S COMING STORY

Jean Paré grew up with an understanding that family, friends and home cooking are the key ingredients for a good life. A mother of four, Jean worked as a professional caterer for 18 years, operating out of her home kitchen. During that time, she came to appreciate quick and easy recipes that call for everyday ingredients. In answer to mounting requests for her recipes, Company's Coming cookbooks were born, and Jean moved on to a new chapter in her career.

In the beginning, Jean worked from a spare bedroom in her home, located in the small prairie town of Vermilion, Alberta, Canada. The first Company's Coming cookbook, *150 Delicious Squares*, was an immediate bestseller. Today, with well over 150 titles in print, Company's Coming has earned the distinction of publishing Canada's most popular cookbooks. The company continues to gain new supporters by adhering to Jean's "Golden Rule of Cooking"— Never share a recipe you wouldn't use yourself. It's an approach that has worked—millions of times over!

Company's Coming cookbooks are distributed throughout Canada, the United States, Australia and other international English-language markets. French and Spanish language editions have also been published. Sales to date have surpassed 25 million copies with no end in sight. Familiar and trusted in home kitchens around the world, Company's Coming cookbooks are highly regarded both as kitchen workbooks and as family heirlooms.

Company's Coming founder Jean Paré

Just as Company's Coming continues to promote the tradition of home cooking, the same is now true with crafting. Like good cooking, great craft results depend upon easy-to-follow instructions, readily available materials and enticing photographs of the finished products. Also like cooking, crafting is meant to be enjoyed in the home or cottage. Company's Coming Crafts, then, is a natural extension from the kitchen into the family room or den.

Because Company's Coming operates a test kitchen and not a craft shop, we've partnered with a major North American craft content publisher to assemble a variety of craft compilations exclusively for us. Our editors have been involved every step of the way. You can see the excellent results for yourself in the book you're holding.

Company's Coming Crafts are for everyone— whether you're a beginner or a seasoned pro. What better gift could you offer than something you've made yourself? In these hectic days, people still enjoy crafting parties; they bring family and friends together in the same way a good meal does. Company's Coming is proud to support crafters with this new creative book series.

We hope you enjoy these easy-to-follow, informative and colourful books, and that they inspire your creativity! So, don't delay—get crafty!

TABLE OF CONTENTS

Between the Covers 6 • Foreword 7 • General Instructions 8

**Patchwork Quilt
Afghan, page 52**

**Midnight Magic
Throw, page 40**

**For the Man,
page 140**

**Paris Stitch Captivating
Capelet, page 72**

**Watermelon Print Throw,
page 36**

TABLE OF CONTENTS

Autumn Wrap, page 78

Baby Burrito Blanket,
page 125

Fallen Petals,
page 142

Spellbinding,
page 139

Shadow Box Trellis,
page 128

Between the Covers

Beading
Beautiful Accessories in Under an Hour

Beading has never been more popular, even though it is a centuries-old art form. Complement your wardrobe, give your home extra flair or add an extra-special personal touch to gifts with these quick and easy beading projects. From gorgeous beaded showpieces to complete jewelry sets, you can create many of these season-by-season projects in less than an hour. With *Beading* as your guide, you can craft beautiful accessories year-round—and have lots of fun doing it!

◄ Refined Glamour, page 94

Crocheting
Easy Blankets, Throws & Wraps

Whether you're a stitching expert or complete novice, *Crocheting* offers page after page of inspiration. Find projects perfect for decorating your home, for looking great while staying warm or for giving that one-of-a-kind gift. Step-by-step instructions, basic tutorials for beginners and a range of simple but stunning projects make crocheting quick, easy and entertaining. Once you start, you'll be hooked!

◄ Gramma & Grandbabies, page 60

Sewing
Fun Weekend Projects

What do you get when you take a sewing machine, a weekend and this collection of fun projects? How about a table runner, bread basket, baby blanket, sewing caddy, shoulder bag or decorative cushion? *Sewing* offers a wide assortment of easy and attractive projects to help you create practical storage solutions, decorations for any room or just the right gift for that someone special. Make it fast and make it special with great designs from *Sewing*.

◄ Pillow Trio, page 102

Also look for Company's Coming *Card Making*, *Knitting* and *Patchwork Quilting* craft books.

For more information about Company's Coming craft books, visit our website, www.companyscoming.com

FOREWORD

Crochet is unique among many other needlecrafts in that no machine can reproduce its stitches—they can only be created by hand, one by one. A crocheted afghan is an expression of love that brings beauty to the home and comforting warmth to the body and soul.

As you peruse these pages, you'll find yourself embarking on an inspired crochet journey through a treasure trove of beautiful and innovative afghans, throws and wraps. From classic favourites to the latest styles, this eclectic collection offers the perfect design for every occasion and personal taste.

Because crocheted afghans are enjoyed all year round, our tantalizing selection of seasonal delights offers a variety of patterns from light and airy to plush and warm. If your sense of style caters to the contemporary, our chic, decorator throws offer a diverse mix of classy designs that fit easily in any setting, from small and cozy to spacious and grand.

And who doesn't love the feel of a cozy, crocheted wrap when the air is chilly? With styles ranging from moderate shoulder toppers to blanket-size coats, our wonderful wraps have got you covered from the minimum to the max.

For any new mom, the gift of a soft, cuddly blanket to welcome her bundle of joy is always a winning choice. Our sweet assortment of baby afghans features a tempting variety of colours and patterns to create charming, one-of-a-kind gifts.

Whether you crochet the delightful projects in this book as gifts for family and friends, to give to charity, or to snuggle up in for some quiet time alone or with someone special, we think you will find them to be among the most pleasurable patterns you've ever stitched, and the most beautiful designs you've ever enjoyed.

Gossamer Throw, page 130

GENERAL INSTRUCTIONS

Lesson 1: Getting Started

To crochet, you need only a crochet hook, some yarn and a tapestry needle.

Yarn

Yarn comes in many sizes, from fine crochet cotton used for doilies, to wonderful bulky mohairs used for afghans and sweaters. The most commonly used yarn is medium (or worsted) weight. It is readily available in a wide variety of beautiful colours. This is the weight we will use in our lessons. Always read yarn labels carefully. The label will tell you how much yarn, in ounces, grams, meters and/or yards, is in the skein or ball. Read the label to find out the fibre content of the yarn, its washability, and sometimes, how to pull the yarn from the skein.

A dye-lot number on the label assures you that the colour of each skein with this number is the same. Yarn of the same colour name may vary in shade somewhat from dye lot to dye lot, creating colour variations in a completed project. Therefore, when purchasing yarn for a project, it is important to match the dye-lot numbers on the skeins.

You'll need a blunt-pointed size 16 steel tapestry needle with an eye big enough to carry the yarn for weaving in yarn ends and sewing seams. You can buy big plastic yarn needles, but they are not as good as the steel needles.

Hooks

Crochet hooks come in many sizes, from very fine steel hooks, used to make intricate doilies and lace, to very large ones of plastic or wood, used to make bulky sweaters or rugs.

The hooks you will use most often are made of aluminum, are about 6 inches long and are sized alphabetically by letter from B (the smallest) to K. For our lessons, you'll need a medium-size H hook.

The aluminum crochet hook looks like this:

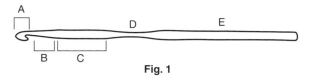

Fig. 1

In Fig. 1, *(A)* is the hook end, which is used to hook the yarn and draw it through other loops of yarn (called stitches). *(B)* is the throat, a shaped area that helps you slide the stitch up onto *(C)* the working area. *(D)* is the fingerhold, a flattened area that helps you grip the hook comfortably; and *(E)* is the handle, which provides balance for easy, smooth work.

It is important that every stitch is made on the working area, never on the throat (which would make the stitch too tight) and never on the fingerhold (which would stretch the stitch).

The hook is held in the right hand, with the thumb and third finger on the fingerhold, and the index finger near the tip of the hook *(Fig. 2)*.

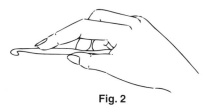

Fig. 2

The hook should be turned slightly toward you, not facing up or down. Fig. 3 shows how the hook is held, viewing from underneath the hand. The hook should be held firmly, but not tightly.

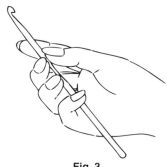

Fig. 3

Lesson 2: Chain Stitch (abbreviated ch)

Crochet usually begins with a series of chain stitches called a beginning or foundation chain. Begin by making a slip knot on the hook about 6 inches from the free end of the yarn. Loop the yarn as shown in Fig. 4.

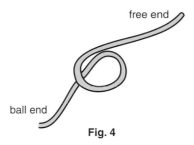

Fig. 4

Insert the hook through centre of loop and hook the free end (Fig. 5).

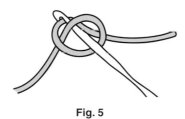

Fig. 5

Pull this through and up onto the working area of the hook (Fig. 6).

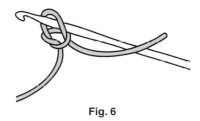

Fig. 6

Pull the free yarn end to tighten the loop (Fig. 7).

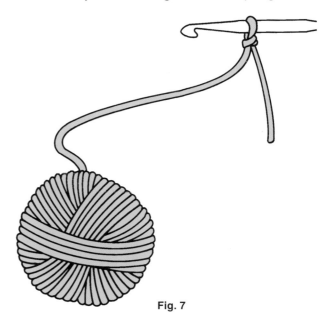

Fig. 7

It should be firm, but loose enough to slide back and forth easily on the hook. Be sure you still have about a 6-inch yarn end.

Hold the hook, now with its slip knot, in your right hand (Fig. 8).

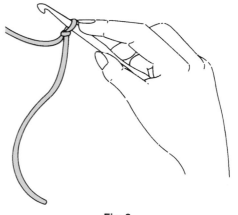

Fig. 8

Now let's make the first chain stitch.

Step 1: Hold the base of the slip knot with the thumb and index finger of your left hand, and thread yarn from the skein over the middle finger *(Fig. 9)* and under the remaining fingers of the left hand *(Fig. 9a)*.

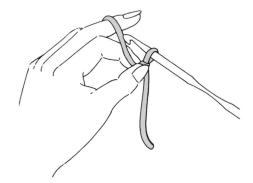

Fig. 9

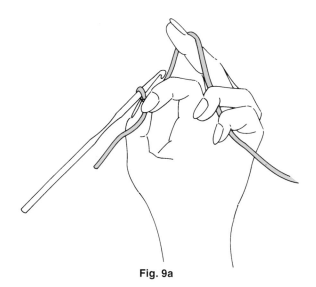

Fig. 9a

Your middle finger will stick up a bit to help the yarn feed smoothly from the skein; the other fingers help maintain even tension on the yarn as you work.

Hint: As you practice, you can adjust the way your left hand holds the thread to however is most comfortable for you.

Step 2: Bring the yarn over the hook from back to front and hook it *(Fig. 10)*.

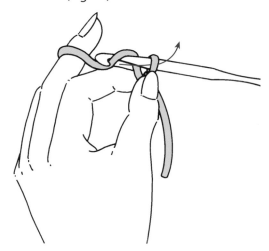

Fig. 10

Draw hooked yarn through the loop of the slip knot on the hook and up onto the working area of the hook *(see arrow on Fig. 10)*; you have now made one chain stitch *(Fig. 11)*.

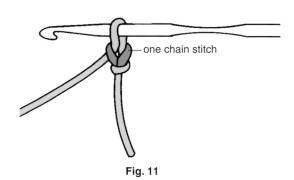

—one chain stitch

Fig. 11

Step 3: Again bring the yarn over the hook from back to front *(Fig. 12a)*.

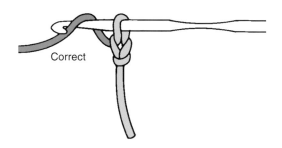

Correct

Fig. 12a

Note: *Take care not to bring yarn from front to back (Fig. 12b).*

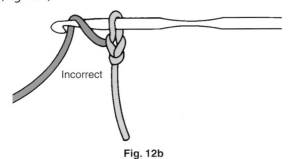

Incorrect

Fig. 12b

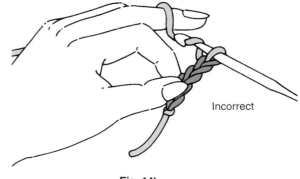

Incorrect

Fig. 14b

Hook it and draw through loop on the hook: You have made another chain stitch *(Fig. 13)*.

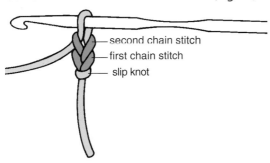

— second chain stitch
— first chain stitch
— slip knot

Fig. 13

Repeat Step 3 for each additional chain stitch, being careful to move the left thumb and index finger up the chain close to the hook after each new stitch or two *(Fig. 14a)*. This helps you control the work. **Note:** *Fig 14b shows the incorrect way to hold the stitches.* Also be sure to pull each new stitch up onto the working area of the hook.

The working yarn and the work in progress are always held in your left hand.

Practice making chains until you are comfortable with your grip on the hook and the flow of the yarn. In the beginning your work will be uneven, with some chain stitches loose and others tight. While you're learning, try to keep the chain

stitches loose. As your skill increases, the chain should be firm, but not tight, with all chain stitches even in size.

Hint: As you practice, if the hook slips out of a stitch, don't get upset! Just insert the hook again from the front into the centre of the last stitch, taking care not to twist the loop *(Fig. 15)*.

When you are comfortable with the chain stitch, draw your hook out of the last stitch and pull out the work back to the beginning. Now you've learned the important first step of crochet: the beginning chain.

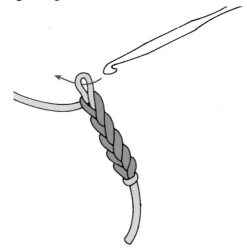

Fig. 15

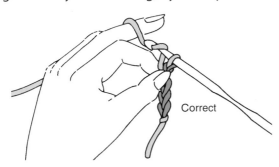

Correct

Fig. 14a

Lesson 3: Working Into the Chain

Once you have worked the beginning chain, you are ready to begin the stitches required to make any project. These stitches are worked into the foundation chain. For practice, make six chains loosely.

Hint: When counting your chain stitches at the start of a pattern—which you must do very carefully before continuing—note that the loop on the hook is never counted as a stitch, and the starting slip knot is never counted as a stitch *(Fig. 16)*.

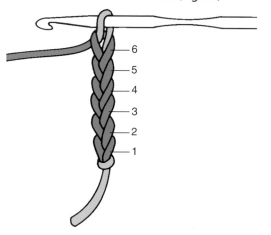

Fig. 16

Now stop and look at the chain. The front looks like a series of interlocking V's *(Fig. 16)*, and each stitch has a bump or ridge at the back *(Fig. 17)*.

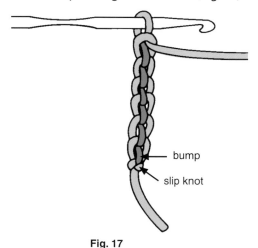

Fig. 17

You will never work into the first chain from the hook. Depending on the stitch, you will work into the second, third, fourth, etc., chain from the hook. The instructions will always state how many chains to skip before starting the first stitch.

When working a stitch, insert hook from the front of the chain, through the centre of a V-stitch and under the corresponding bump on the back of the same stitch *(Fig. 18)*.

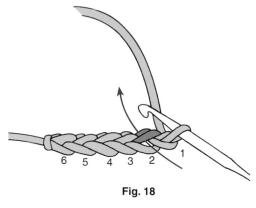

Fig. 18

Excluding the first stitch, you will work into every stitch in the chain unless the pattern states differently, but not into the starting slip knot *(Fig. 18a)*. Be sure that you do not skip that last chain at the end.

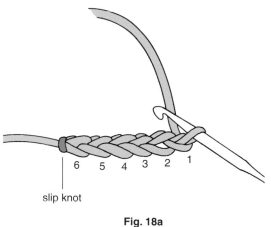

Fig. 18a

Lesson 4: Single Crochet (abbreviated sc)

Most crochet is made with variations of just four different stitches: single crochet, double crochet, half double crochet and treble crochet. The stitches differ mainly in height, which is varied by the number of times the yarn is wrapped around the hook. The shortest and most basic of these stitches is the single crochet.

Working Row 1

To practice, begin with the chain of six stitches made in Lesson 3 and work the first row of single crochet as follows:

Step 1: Skip first chain stitch from hook. Insert hook in the second chain stitch through the centre of the V and under the back bump; with third finger of your left hand, bring yarn over the hook from back to front, and hook the yarn (Fig.19).

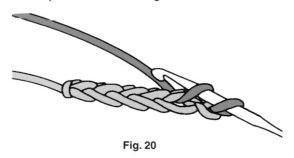

Fig. 19

Draw yarn through the chain stitch and well up onto the working area of the hook. You now have two loops on the hook (Fig. 20).

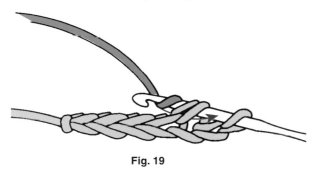

Fig. 20

Step 2: Again bring yarn over the hook from back to front, hook it and draw it through both loops on the hook (Fig. 21).

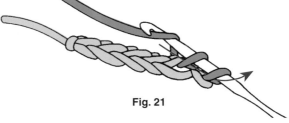

Fig. 21

One loop will remain on the hook, and you have made one single crochet (Fig. 22).

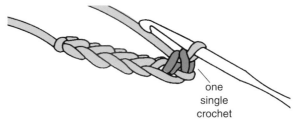

one single crochet

Fig. 22

Step 3: Insert hook in next chain stitch as before, hook the yarn and draw it through the chain stitch; hook the yarn again and draw it through both loops: You have made another single crochet.

Repeat Step 3 in each remaining chain stitch, taking care to work in the last chain stitch, **but not in the slip knot**. You have completed one row of single crochet, and should have five stitches in the row. Fig. 23 shows how to count the stitches.

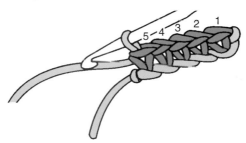

Fig. 23

Hint: As you work, be careful not to twist the chain; keep all the V's facing you.

Working Row 2

To work the second row of single crochet, you need to turn the work in the direction of the arrow (counterclockwise), as shown in Fig. 24, so you can work back across the first row.

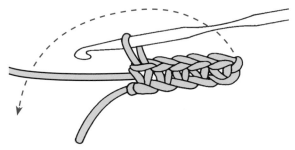

Fig. 24

Do not remove the hook from the loop as you do this (*Fig. 24a*).

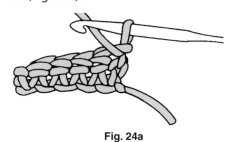

Fig. 24a

Now you need to bring the yarn up to the correct height to work the first stitch. So, to raise the yarn, chain one (*this is called a beginning or a turning chain*).

This row, and all the following rows of single crochet, will be worked into a previous row of single crochet, not into the beginning chain as you did before. Remember that when you worked into the starting chain, you inserted the hook through the centre of the V and under the bump. This is only done when working into a starting chain.

To work into a previous row of crochet, insert the hook under both loops of the previous stitch, as shown in Fig. 25, instead of through the centre of the V.

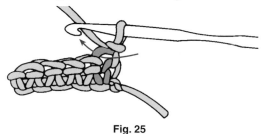

Fig. 25

The first single crochet of the row is worked in the last stitch of the previous row (*Fig. 25*), not into the turning chain. Work a single crochet into each single crochet to the end, taking care to work in each stitch, especially the last stitch, which is easy to miss (*Fig. 26*).

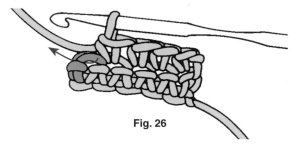

Fig. 26

Stop now and count your stitches; you should still have five single crochets on the row (*Fig. 27*).

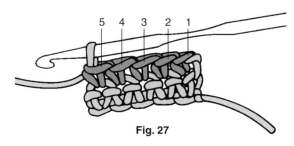

Fig. 27

Hint: When you want to pause to count stitches, check your work, have a snack or chat on the phone, you can remove your hook from the work—but do this at the end of a row, not in the middle. To remove the hook, pull straight up on the hook to make a long loop (*Fig. 28*). Then withdraw the hook and put it on a table or other safe place (sofas and chairs have a habit of eating crochet hooks). Put work in a safe place so loop is not pulled out. To begin work again, just insert the hook in the big loop (*don't twist the loop*), and pull on the yarn from the skein to tighten the loop.

To end row two, after the last single crochet, turn the work counterclockwise.

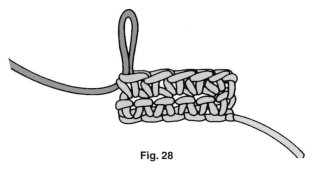

Fig. 28

Here is the way instructions for row two might be written in a pattern:
Note: *To save space, a number of abbreviations are used. For a list of abbreviations used in patterns, see page 31.*

Row 2: Ch 1, sc in each sc, turn.

Working Row 3

Row 3 is worked exactly as you worked row 2. Here are the instructions as they would be given in a pattern:
Row 3: Rep row 2.
Now wasn't that easy? For practice, work three more rows, which means you will repeat row 2 three times more.

> **Hint:** Try to keep your stitches as smooth and even as possible; remember to work loosely rather than tightly and to make each stitch well up on the working area of the hook. Be sure to turn at the end of each row and to check carefully to be sure you've worked into the last stitch of each row.

> Count the stitches at the end of each row; do you still have five? Good work.

> **Hint:** What if you don't have five stitches at the end of a row? Perhaps you worked two stitches in one stitch, or skipped a stitch. Find your mistake, then just pull out your stitches back to the mistake; pulling out in crochet is simple. Just take out the hook and gently pull on the yarn. The stitches will come out easily; when you reach the place where you want to start again, insert the hook in the last loop *(taking care not to twist it)* and begin.

Fastening Off

It's time to move on to another stitch, so let's fasten off your single crochet practice piece, which you can keep for future reference. After the last stitch of the last row, cut the yarn, leaving a 6-inch end. As you did when you took your hook out for a break, draw the hook straight up, but this time draw the yarn cut end completely through the stitch. Photo A shows an actual sample of six rows of single crochet to which you can compare your practice rows. It also shows how to count the stitches and rows.

Now you can put the piece away, and it won't pull out *(you might want to tag this piece as a sample of single crochet)*.

Photo A

Lesson 5: Double Crochet

(abbreviated dc)

Double crochet is a taller stitch than single crochet. To practice, first chain 14 stitches loosely. Then work the first row of double crochet as follows:

Working Row 1

Step 1: Bring yarn once over the hook from back to front *(as though you were going to make another chain stitch)*; skip the first three chains from the hook, then insert hook in the fourth chain *(Fig. 29)*.

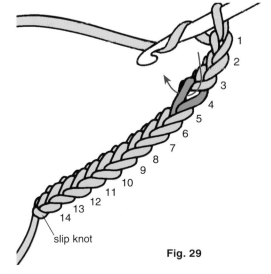

slip knot

Fig. 29

Remember not to count the loop on the hook as a chain. Be sure to go through the centre of the V of the chain and under the bump at the back, and do not twist the chain.

Step 2: Hook yarn and draw it through the chain stitch and up onto the working area of the hook: you now have three loops on the hook *(Fig. 30)*.

Fig. 30

Step 3: Hook yarn and draw through the first 2 loops on the hook *(Fig. 31)*.

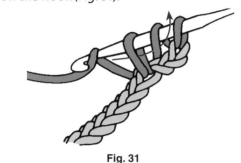

Fig. 31

You now have 2 loops on the hook *(Fig. 32)*.

Fig. 32

Step 4: Hook yarn and draw through both loops on the hook *(Fig. 33)*.

Fig. 33

You have now completed one double crochet and one loop remains on the hook *(Fig. 34)*.

one double crochet

Fig. 34

Repeat Steps 1 through 4 in each chain stitch across *(except in Step 1, work in next chain; don't skip three chains)*.

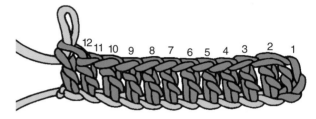

Fig. 35

When you've worked a double crochet in the last chain, pull out your hook and look at your work. Then count your double crochet stitches: There should be 12 of them, counting the first three chain stitches you skipped at the beginning of the row as a double crochet *(Fig. 35)*.

Hint: In working double crochet on a beginning chain row, the three chains skipped before making the first double crochet are always counted as a double crochet stitch.

Turn the work counterclockwise before beginning row 2.

Working Row 2

To work row 2, you need to bring the thread up to the correct height for the next row. To raise the yarn, chain three *(this is called the beginning or the turning chain)*.

The three chains in the turning chain just made count as the first double crochet of the new row, so skip the first double crochet and work a double crochet in the second stitch. Be sure to insert hook under top two loops of stitch: Figs. 36a and 36b indicate the correct and incorrect placement of this stitch.

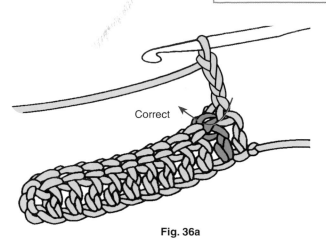

Fig. 36a

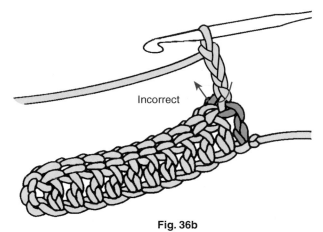

Fig. 36b

Work a double crochet in each remaining stitch across the previous row; at the end of each row, be sure to work the last double crochet in the top of the turning chain from the previous row. Be sure to insert hook in the centre of the V (and back bump) of the top chain of the turning chain *(Fig. 37)*. Stop and count your double crochets; there should be 12 stitches. Now, turn.

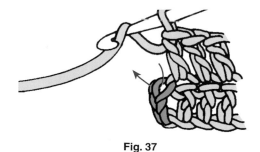

Fig. 37

Here is the way the instructions might be written in a pattern:
Row 2: Ch 3, dc in each dc, turn. *(12 dc)*

Working Row 3

Row 3 is worked exactly as you worked row 2. In a pattern, instructions would read:
Row 3: Rep row 2.
For practice, work three more rows, repeating row 2. At the end of the last row, fasten off the yarn as you did for the single crochet practice piece. Photo B shows a sample of six rows of double crochet and how to count the stitches and rows.

Photo B

Break Time!

Now you have learned the two stitches used most often in crochet. Since you've worked so hard, it's time to take a break. Walk around, relax your hands, have a snack or just take a few minutes to release the stress that sometimes develops when learning something new.

Lesson 6: Half Double Crochet
(abbreviated hdc)

Just as its name implies, this stitch eliminates one step of double crochet and works up about half as tall. To practice, chain 13 stitches loosely.

Working Row 1
Step 1: Bring yarn once over hook from back to front, skip the first two chains, then insert hook in the third chain from the hook (*Fig. 38*).

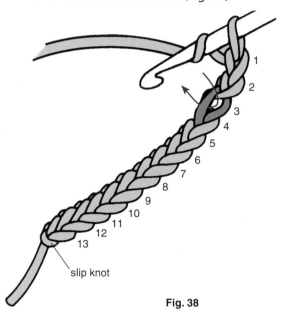

Fig. 38

Remember not to count the loop on the hook as a chain.
Step 2: Hook yarn and draw it through the chain stitch and up onto the working area of the hook. You now have three loops on the hook (*Fig. 39*).

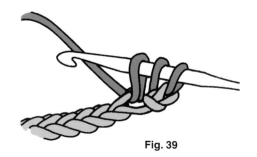

Fig. 39

Step 3: Hook yarn and draw it through all three loops on the hook in one motion (*Fig. 40*).

Fig. 40

You have completed one half double crochet and one loop remains on the hook (*Fig. 41*).

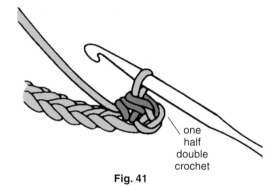

Fig. 41

In next chain stitch, work a half double crochet as follows:
Step 1: Bring yarn once over hook from back to front, insert hook in next chain.
Step 2: Hook yarn and draw it through the chain stitch and up onto the working area of the hook. You now have three loops on the hook.
Step 3: Hook yarn and draw it through all three loops on the hook in one motion.
Repeat the previous three steps in each remaining

chain stitch across. Stop and count your stitches: You should have 12 half double crochets, counting the first two chains you skipped at the beginning of the row as a half double crochet *(Fig. 42)*.

Fig. 42

Turn your work.

Working Row 2

Like double crochet, the turning chain counts as a stitch in half double crochet (unless your pattern specifies otherwise). Chain two, skip the first half double crochet of the previous row and work a half double crochet in the second stitch *(Fig. 43)* and in each remaining stitch across the previous row. At the end of the row, chain two and turn.

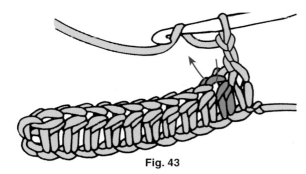

Fig. 43

Here is the way the instructions might be written in a pattern:

Row 2: Ch 2, hdc in each hdc, turn. *(12 hdc)*

Working Row 3

Row 3 is worked exactly as you worked row 2.

For practice, work three more rows, repeating row 2. Be sure to count your stitches carefully at the end of each row. When the practice rows are completed, fasten off. Photo C shows a sample of six rows of half double crochet and how to count the stitches and the rows. Continue with the next lesson.

Photo C

Lesson 7: Treble Crochet
(abbreviated tr)

Treble crochet is a tall stitch that works up quickly and is fun to do. To practice, first chain 15 stitches loosely. Then work the first row as follows:

Working Row 1

Step 1: Bring yarn twice over the hook (from back to front), skip the first four chains, then insert hook into the fifth chain from the hook *(Fig. 44)*.

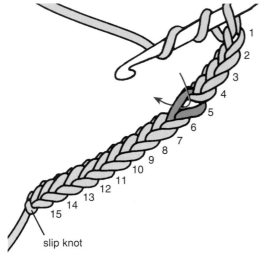

slip knot

Fig. 44

Step 2: Hook yarn and draw it through the chain stitch and up onto the working area of the hook; you now have four loops on the hook *(Fig. 45)*.

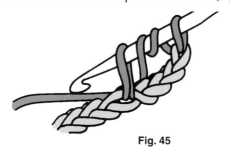

Fig. 45

Step 3: Hook yarn and draw it through the first two loops on the hook *(Fig. 46)*.

Fig. 46

You now have three loops on the hook *(Fig. 46a)*.

Fig. 46a

Step 4: Hook yarn again and draw it through the next two loops on the hook *(Fig. 47)*.

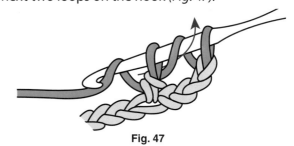

Fig. 47

Two loops remain on the hook *(Fig. 47a)*.

Fig. 47a

Step 5: Hook yarn and draw it through both remaining loops on the hook *(Fig 48)*.

Fig. 48

You have now completed one treble crochet and one loop remains on the hook *(Fig. 49)*.

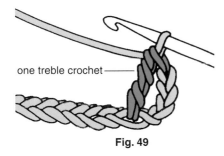

one treble crochet

Fig. 49

In next chain stitch work a treble crochet as follows:
Step 1: Bring yarn twice over the hook (from back to front); insert hook in the next chain *(Fig. 50)*.

Fig. 50

Step 2: Hook yarn and draw it through the chain stitch and up onto the working area of the hook; you now have four loops on the hook.
Step 3: Hook yarn and draw it through the first two loops on the hook.
You now have three loops on the hook.
Step 4: Hook yarn again and draw it through the next two loops on the hook.
Two loops remain on the hook.
Step 5: Hook yarn and draw it through both remaining loops on the hook.

Repeat the previous five steps in each remaining chain stitch across.

When you've worked a treble crochet in the last chain, count your stitches: There should be 12 of them, counting the first four chains you skipped at the beginning of the row as a treble crochet *(Fig. 51)*; turn work.

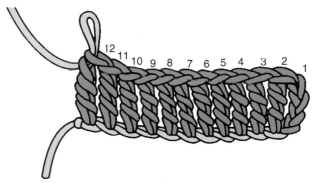

Fig. 51

Hint: In working the first row of treble crochet, the four chains skipped before making the first treble crochet are always counted as a treble crochet stitch.

Working Row 2

Chain four to bring your yarn up to the correct height, and to count as the first stitch of the row. Skip the first stitch and work a treble crochet in the second stitch (*Fig. 52*).

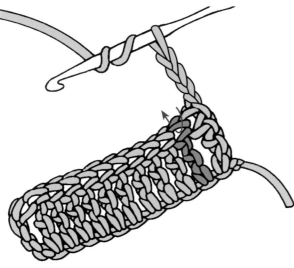

Fig. 52

Work a treble crochet in each remaining stitch across previous row; be sure to work last treble crochet in the top of the turning chain from the previous row. Count stitches: Be sure you still have 12 stitches; turn work.

Hint: Remember to work last treble crochet of each row in turning chain of previous row. Missing this stitch in the turning chain is a common error.

Here is the way the instructions might be written in a pattern:

Row 2: Ch 4, tr in each tr, turn. (*12 tr*)

Working Row 3

Work row 3 exactly as you worked row 2.

For practice, work three more rows, repeating row 2. At the end of the last row, fasten off the yarn. Photo D shows a sample of six rows of treble crochet and how to count the stitches and rows.

Photo D

Lesson 8: Slip Stitch
(abbreviated sl st)

This is the shortest of all crochet stitches and is really more a technique than a stitch. Slip stitches are usually used to move yarn across a group of stitches without adding height, or they may be used to join work.

Moving Yarn Across Stitches
Chain 10.

Working Row 1
Double crochet in the fourth chain from hook (see page 15) and in each chain across. Turn work. On the next row, you are going to slip stitch across the first four stitches before beginning to work double crochet again.

Working Row 2
Instead of making three chains for the turning chain as you would usually do for a second row of double crochet, this time just chain one. The beginning chain-one does not count as a stitch; therefore, insert hook under both loops of first stitch, hook yarn and draw it through both loops of stitch and loop on the hook (Fig 53): one slip stitch made.

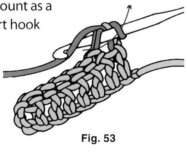

Fig. 53

Work a slip stitch in the same manner in each of the next three stitches. Now we're going to finish the row in double crochet; chain three to get yarn at the right height (the chain-three counts as a double crochet), then work a double crochet in each of the remaining stitches. Look at your work and see how we moved the thread across with slip stitches, adding very little height (Fig. 54). Fasten off and save the sample. Here is the way the instructions might be written in a pattern.

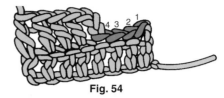

Fig. 54

Row 2: Sl st in next 4 dc; ch 3, dc in each rem dc. (5 dc) Fasten off.

Hint: When slip stitching across stitches, always work very loosely.

Joining Stitches

Joining a chain into a circle.
Chain six, then insert hook through the first chain you made (next to the slip knot—Fig. 55).

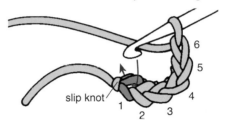

Fig. 55

Hook yarn and draw it through the chain and through the loop on hook; you have now joined the six chains into a circle or a ring. This is the way many motifs, such as granny squares, are started. Cut yarn and keep this practice piece as a sample.

Joining the end of a round to the beginning of the same round.
Chain six; join with a slip stitch in first chain you made to form a ring. Chain three; work 11 double crochet in the ring; insert hook in third chain of beginning chain three (Fig. 56); hook yarn and draw it through

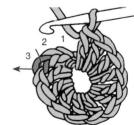

Fig. 56

the chain and through the loop on the hook; you have now joined the round. Cut yarn and keep this piece as a sample. Here is the way the instructions might be written in a pattern:

Rnd 1: Ch 3, 11 dc in ring; join in 3rd ch of beg ch-3.

Lesson 9: Working With Colours

Working with colours often involves reading charts, changing colours, and learning how to carry or pick up colours.

Working From Charts

Charts are easy to work from once you understand how to follow them. When working from a chart, remember that for each odd-numbered row, you will work the chart from right to left, and for each even-numbered row, you will work the chart from left to right.

Odd-numbered rows are worked on the right side of the piece and even-numbered rows are worked on the wrong side. To help follow across the row, you will find it helpful to place a ruler or sheet of paper directly below the row being worked.

Changing Colours

To change from a working colour to a new colour, work the last stitch to be done in the working colour until two loops remain on the hook (Photo A). Draw new colour through the two loops on hook. Drop working colour (Photo B) and continue to work in the new colour. This method can be used when change of colour is at the end of a row or within the row.

Photo B

Carrying Or Picking Up Colours

In some patterns, you may need to carry a colour on the wrong side of the work for several stitches or pickup a colour used on the previous row. To carry a colour means to carry the strand on the wrong side of the work. To prevent having loops of unworked yarn, it is helpful to work over the strand of the carried colour. To do this, consider the strand a part of the stitch being worked into and simply insert the hook in the stitch and draw the new colour through (Photo C). When changing from working colour to a colour that has been carried or used on the previous row, always bring this colour under the working colour. This is very important, as it prevents holes in your work.

Photo A

Photo C

Special Helps

Increasing & Decreasing

Shaping is done by increasing, which adds stitches to make the crocheted piece wider, or decreasing, which subtracts stitches to make the piece narrower.

Note: Make a practice sample by chaining 15 stitches loosely and working four rows of single crochet with 14 stitches in each row. Do not fasten off at end of last row. Use this sample swatch to practice the following method of increasing stitches.

Increasing: To increase one stitch in single, half double, double or treble crochet, simply work two stitches in one stitch. For example, if you are working in single crochet and you need to increase one stitch, you would work one single crochet in the next stitch; then you would work another single crochet in the same stitch.

For practice: On sample swatch, turn work and chain one. Single crochet in first two stitches; increase in next stitch by working two single crochets in stitch *(Fig. 59)*.

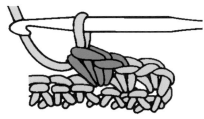

single crochet increase

Fig. 59

Repeat increase in each stitch across row to last two stitches; single crochet in each of next two stitches. Count your stitches: You should have 24 stitches. If you don't have 24 stitches, examine your swatch to see if you have increased in each specified stitch. Rework the row if necessary.

Increases in half double, double and treble crochet are shown in Figs. 59a, 59b and 59c.

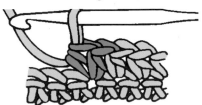

half double crochet increase

Fig. 59a

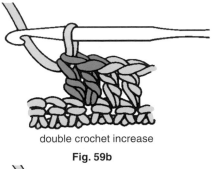

double crochet increase

Fig. 59b

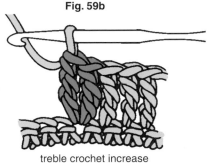

treble crochet increase

Fig. 59c

Note: Make another practice sample by chaining 15 loosely and working four rows of single crochet. Do not fasten off at end of last row. Use this sample swatch to practice the following methods of decreasing stitches.

Decreasing: This is how to work a decrease in the four main stitches. Each decrease gives one fewer stitch than you had before.

Single crochet decrease (sc dec): Insert hook and draw up a loop in each of the next two stitches *(three loops now on hook)*, hook yarn and draw through all three loops on the hook *(Fig. 60)*.

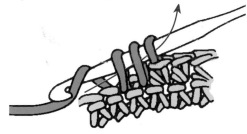

Fig. 60

Single crochet decrease made *(Fig. 61)*.

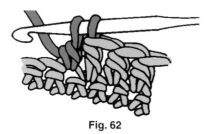

Fig. 61

Double crochet decrease (dc dec): Work a double crochet in the specified stitch until two loops remain on the hook *(Fig. 62)*.

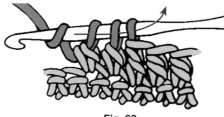

Fig. 62

Keeping these two loops on hook, work another double crochet in the next stitch until three loops remain on hook; hook yarn and draw through all three loops on the hook *(Fig. 63)*.

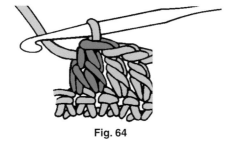

Fig. 63

Double crochet decrease made *(Fig. 64)*.

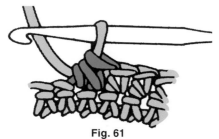

Fig. 64

Half double crochet decrease (hdc dec): Yo, insert hook in specified stitch and draw up a loop: three loops on the hook *(Fig. 65)*.

Fig. 65

Keeping these three loops on hook, yo and draw up a loop in the next stitch *(five loops now on hook)*, hook yarn and draw through all five loops on the hook *(Fig. 66)*.

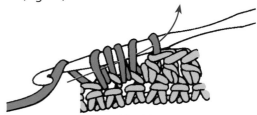

Fig. 66

Half double crochet decrease made *(Fig. 67)*.

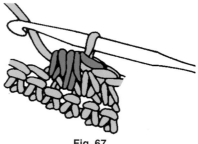

Fig. 67

Treble crochet decrease (tr dec): Work a treble crochet in the specified stitch until two loops remain on the hook *(Fig. 68)*.

Fig. 68

Keeping these two loops on hook, work another triple crochet in the next stitch until 3 loops remain on the hook; hook yarn and draw through all three loops on the hook *(Fig. 69)*.

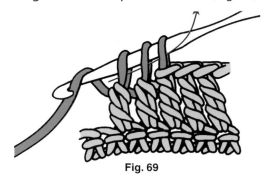

Fig. 69

Treble crochet decrease made *(Fig. 70)*.

Fig. 70

Joining New Thread

Never tie or leave knots! In crochet, yarn ends can be easily worked in and hidden because of the density of the stitches. Always leave at least 6-inch ends when fastening off yarn just used and when joining new yarn. If a flaw or a knot appears in the yarn while you are working from a skein, cut out the imperfection and rejoin the yarn.

Whenever possible, join new yarn at the end of a row. To do this, work the last stitch with the old yarn until two loops remain on the hook, then with the new yarn complete the stitch *(Fig. 71)*.

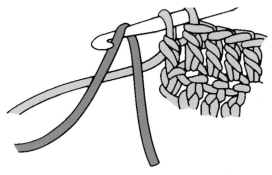

Fig. 71

To join new yarn in the middle of a row, when about 12 inches of the old yarn remains, work several more stitches with the old yarn, working the stitches over the end of new yarn *(Fig. 72 shown in double crochet)*. Then change yarns in stitch as previously explained.

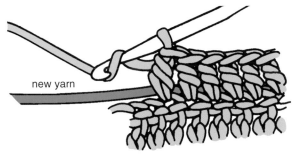

new yarn

Fig. 72

Continuing with the new yarn, work the following stitches over the old yarn end.

Finishing

A carefully crocheted project can be disappointing if the finishing has been done incorrectly. Correct finishing techniques are not difficult, but do require time, attention and a knowledge of basic techniques.

Weaving in ends: The first procedure of finishing is to securely weave in all yarn ends. Thread a size 16 steel tapestry needle with yarn, then weave running stitches either horizontally or vertically on the wrong side of work. First weave about 1 inch in one direction and then ½ inch in the reverse direction. Be sure yarn doesn't show on right side of work. Cut off excess yarn. Never weave in more than one yarn end at a time.

Sewing seams: Edges in crochet are usually butted together for seaming instead of layered, to avoid bulk. Do not sew too tightly—seams should be elastic and have the same stretch as the crocheted pieces.

Carefully matching stitches and rows as much as possible, sew the seams with the same yarn you used when crocheting.

1. Invisible seam: This seam provides a smooth, neat appearance because the edges are woven together invisibly from the right side. Join vertical edges, such as side or sleeve seams, through the matching edge stitches, bringing the yarn up through the posts of the stitches *(Fig. 73)*.

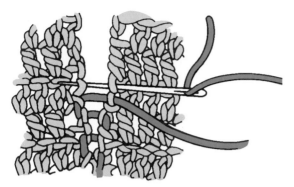

Fig. 73

If a firmer seam is desired, weave the edges together through both the tops and the posts of the matching edge stitches.

2. Backstitch seam: This method gives a strong, firm edge and is used when the seam will have a lot of stress or pull on it. Hold the pieces with right sides together and then sew through both thicknesses as shown (*Fig. 74*).

Fig. 74

3. Overcast seam: Strips and pieces of afghans are frequently joined in this manner. Hold the pieces with right sides together and overcast edges, carefully matching stitches on the two pieces (*Fig. 75*).

Fig. 75

Edges can also be joined in this manner, using only the back loops or the front loops of each stitch (see page 28).

4. Crocheted Seam: Holding pieces with right sides together, join yarn with a slip stitch at right-side edge. Loosely slip stitch pieces together, being sure not to pull stitches too tightly (*Fig. 76*). You

may wish to use a hook one size larger than the one used in the project.

Fig. 76

Edging

Single crochet edging: A row of single crochet worked around a competed project gives a finished look. The instructions will say to "work a row of single crochet, taking care to keep work flat." This means you need to adjust your stitches as you work. To work the edging, insert hook from front to back through the edge stitch and work a single crochet. Continue evenly along the edge. You may need to skip a row or a stitch here or there to keep the edging from rippling, or add a stitch to keep the work from pulling.

When working around a corner, it is usually necessary to work at least three stitches in the corner centre stitch to keep the corner flat and square (*Fig. 77*).

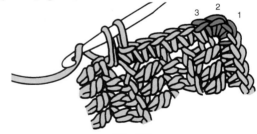

Fig. 77

Reverse single crochet edging: A single crochet edging is sometimes worked from left to right for a more dominant edge. To work reverse single crochet, insert hook in stitch to the right (*Fig. 78*), hook yarn and draw through stitch, hook yarn and draw through both loops on the hook (*Fig. 79*).

Fig. 78

Fig. 79

Gauge

We've left this until last, but it really is the single most important thing in crochet.

If you don't work to gauge, your crocheted projects may not be the correct size, and you may not have enough yarn to finish your project.

Gauge means the number of stitches per inch and rows per inch that result from a specified yarn worked with a specified-size hook. Since everyone crochets differently—some loosely, some tightly, some in-between—the measurements of individual work can vary greatly when using the same-size hook and yarn. It is **your responsibility** to make sure you achieve the gauge specified in the pattern.

Hook sizes given in instructions are merely guides and should never be used without making a 4-inch-square sample swatch to check gauge.

Make the sample gauge swatch using the size hook, and the yarn and stitch specified in the pattern. If you have more stitches per inch than specified, try again using a larger-size hook. If you have fewer stitches per inch than specified, try again using a smaller-size hook. Do not hesitate to change to a larger- or smaller-size hook, if necessary, to achieve gauge.

If you have the correct number of stitches per inch, but cannot achieve the row gauge, adjust the height of your stitches. This means that after inserting the hook to begin a new stitch, draw up a little more yarn if your stitches are not tall enough—this makes the first loop slightly higher; or draw up less yarn if your stitches are too tall. Practice will help you achieve the correct height.

This photo shows how to measure your gauge.

Metric Chart

INCHES INTO MILLIMETERS & CENTIMETERS (Rounded off slightly)

inches	mm	cm	inches	cm	inches	cm	inches	cm
1/8	3	0.3	5	12.5	21	53.5	38	96.5
1/4	6	0.6	5 1/2	14	22	56	39	99
3/8	10	1	6	15	23	58.5	40	101.5
1/2	13	1.3	7	18	24	61	41	104
5/8	15	1.5	8	20.5	25	63.5	42	106.5
3/4	20	2	9	23	26	66	43	109
7/8	22	2.2	10	25.5	27	68.5	44	112
1	25	2.5	11	28	28	71	45	114.5
1 1/4	32	3.2	12	30.5	29	73.5	46	117
1 1/2	38	3.8	13	33	30	76	47	119.5
1 3/4	45	4.5	14	35.5	31	79	48	122
2	50	5	15	38	32	81.5	49	124.5
2 1/2	65	6.5	16	40.5	33	84	50	127
3	75	7.5	17	43	34	86.5		
3 1/2	90	9	18	46	35	89		
4	100	10	19	48.5	36	91.5		
4 1/2	115	11.5	20	51	37	94		

CROCHET HOOKS CONVERSION CHART

U.S.	1/B	2/C	3/D	4/E	5/F	6/G	8/H	9/I	10/J	10½/K	N
Continental-mm	2.25	2.75	3.25	3.5	3.75	4.25	5	5.5	6	6.5	9.0

STEEL THREAD HOOKS METRIC CONVERSION CHART

U.S.	16	14	13	12	11	10	9	8	7	6	5	4	3	2	1	0	00
U.K.	-	7	6½	6	5½	5	4	3	2½	2	1½	1	1/0	2/0	3/0	00	-
Metric-mm	0.6	0.75	0.85	1.00	1.10	1.15	1.25	1.50	1.65	1.80	1.90	2.00	2.10	2.20	2.25	2.50	2.70

Standard Yarn Weight System

Categories of yarn, gauge ranges, and recommended needle and hook sizes

Yarn Weight Symbol & Category Names	1 SUPER FINE	2 FINE	3 LIGHT	4 MEDIUM	5 BULKY	6 SUPER BULKY
Type of Yarns in Category	Sock, Fingering, Baby	Sport, Baby	DK, Light Worsted	Worsted, Afghan, Aran	Chunky, Craft, Rug	Bulky, Roving
Knit Gauge Range* in Stockinette Stitch to 4 inches	27–32 sts	23–26 sts	21–24 sts	16–20 sts	12–15 sts	6–11 sts
Recommended Needle in Metric Size Range	2.25–3.25 mm	3.25–3.75 mm	3.75–4.5 mm	4.5–5.5 mm	5.5–8 mm	8 mm and larger
Recommended Needle U.S. Size Range	1 to 3	3 to 5	5 to 7	7 to 9	9 to 11	11 and larger
Crochet Gauge* Ranges in Single Crochet to 4 inch	21–32 sts	16–20 sts	12–17 sts	11–14 sts	8–11 sts	5–9 sts
Recommended Hook in Metric Size Range	2.25–3.5 mm	3.5–4.5 mm	4.5–5.5 mm	5.5–6.5 mm	6.5–9 mm	9 mm and larger
Recommended Hook U.S. Size Range	B1–E4	E4–7	7–I9	I-9–K-10½	K-10½–M-13	M-13 and larger

* GUIDELINES ONLY: The above reflect the most commonly used gauges and needle or hook sizes for specific yarn categories.

Skill Levels

BEGINNER

Beginner projects for first-time crocheters using basic stitches. Minimal shaping.

EASY

Easy projects using basic stitches, repetitive stitch patterns, simple colour changes and simple shaping and finishing.

INTERMEDIATE

Intermediate projects with a variety of stitches, mid-level shaping and finishing.

EXPERIENCED

Experienced projects using advanced techniques and stitches, detailed shaping and refined finishing.

Stitch Guide

ABBREVIATIONS

beg	begin/begins/beginning
bpdc	back post double crochet
bpsc	back post single crochet
bptr	back post treble crochet
CC	contrasting colour
ch(s)	chain(s)
ch-	refers to chain or space previously made (i.e. ch-1 space)
ch sp(s)	chain space(s)
cl(s)	cluster(s)
cm	centimetre(s)
dc	double crochet (singular/plural)
dc dec	double crochet 2 or more stitches together, as indicated
dec	decrease/decreases/decreasing
dtr	double treble crochet
ext	extended
fpdc	front post double crochet
fpsc	front post single crochet
fptr	front post treble crochet
g	gram(s)
hdc	half double crochet
hdc dec	half double crochet 2 or more stitches together, as indicated
inc	increase/increases/increasing
lp(s)	loop(s)
MC	main colour
mm	millimetre(s)
oz	ounce(s)
pc	popcorn(s)
rem	remain/remains/remaining
rep(s)	repeat(s)
rnd(s)	round(s)
RS	right side
sc	single crochet (singular/plural)
sc dec	single crochet 2 or more stitches together, as indicated
sk	skip/skipped/skipping
sl st(s)	slip stitch(es)
sp(s)	space(s)/spaced
st(s)	stitch(es)
tog	together
tr	treble crochet
trtr	triple treble
WS	wrong side
yd(s)	yard(s)
yo	yarn over

Chain—ch: Yo, pull through lp on hook.

Slip stitch—sl st: Insert hook in st, yo, pull through both lps on hook.

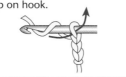

Single crochet—sc: Insert hook in st, yo, pull through st, yo, pull through both lps on hook.

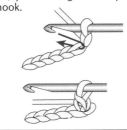

Front loop—front lp
Back loop—back lp

Front Loop   Back Loop

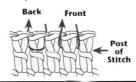

Front post stitch—fp:
Back post stitch—bp: When working post st, insert hook from right to left around post st on previous row.

Back   Front

Post of Stitch

Half double crochet—hdc: Yo, insert hook in st, yo, pull through st, yo, pull through all 3 lps on hook.

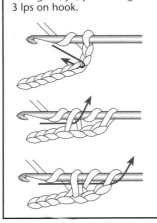

Double crochet—dc: Yo, insert hook in st, yo, pull through st, [yo, pull through 2 lps] twice.

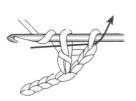

Change colours: Drop first colour; with 2nd colour, pull through last 2 lps of st.

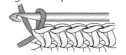

Treble crochet—tr: Yo 2 times, insert hook in st, yo, pull through st, [yo, pull through 2 lps] 3 times.

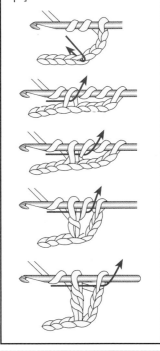

Double treble crochet—dtr: Yo 3 times, insert hook in st, yo, pull through st, [yo, pull through 2 lps] 4 times.

Single crochet decrease (sc dec): (Insert hook, yo, draw up a lp) in each of the sts indicated, yo, draw through all lps on hook.

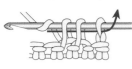

Example of 2-sc dec

Half double crochet decrease (hdc dec): (Yo, insert hook, yo, draw lp through) in each of the sts indicated, yo, draw through all lps on hook.

Example of 2-hdc dec

Double crochet decrease (dc dec): (Yo, insert hook, yo, draw lp through, yo, draw through 2 lps on hook) in each of the sts indicated, yo, draw through all lps on hook.

Example of 2-dc dec

Example of 2-tr dec

Treble crochet decrease (tr dec): Holding back last lp of each st, tr in each of the sts indicated, yo, pull through all lps on hook.

US		UK
sl st (slip stitch)	=	sc (single crochet)
sc (single crochet)	=	dc (double crochet)
hdc (half double crochet)	=	htr (half treble crochet)
dc (double crochet)	=	tr (treble crochet)
tr (treble crochet)	=	dtr (double treble crochet)
dtr (double treble crochet)	=	ttr (triple treble crochet)
skip	=	miss

Modern Day Warmth Sofa Afghan

Stripes of dimensional stitches give rich texture and eye-catching style to this contemporary design.

DESIGN BY ZELDA WORKMAN

Skill Level

INTERMEDIATE

Finished Size

Approximately 54 x 66 inches

Materials

- Red Heart Plush medium (worsted) weight yarn: 24oz/1160yds/672g each #9628 dark sage (A) and #9104 taupe (B)
- Size H/8/5mm crochet hook or size needed to obtain gauge
- Tapestry needle

Gauge

13 sts = 4 inches

Special Stitches

Beginning extended stitch (beg ext st): Yo, insert hook in next ch-1 sp, pull up a lp, working around ch-1 sts made in previous rows, [yo, insert hook from front to back around ch st of row below, pull up a lp] 10 times, yo, insert hook from front to back around ch st of foundation ch, pull up a lp, [yo, pull through 2 lps on hook] 22 times.

Extended stitch (ext st): Yo,

insert hook in next ch-1 sp, pull up a lp, working around ch-1 sts made in previous rows, [yo, insert hook from front to back around ch st of row below, pull up a lp] 8 times, yo, insert hook in top of ext st in next row, pull up a lp, insert hook around post of same ext st, pull up a lp, [yo, pull through 2 lps on hook] 22 times.

Afghan

Centre

Row 1 (RS): With B, ch 166, dc in 4th ch from hook and in next 2 chs, [ch 1, sk next ch, dc in next 4 ch] across, turn. *(163 sts)*

Row 2: Ch 3 *(counts as a dc now and throughout)*, dc in next 3 dc, [ch 1, sk next ch, dc in next 4 dc] across, turn.

Rows 3–10: Rep row 2, changing to A at end of row 10.

Row 11: Ch 3, dc in next 3 dc, [**beg ext st** *(see Special Stitches)* over next vertical row of ch-1 sps, dc in next 4 dc] across, turn.

Row 12: Ch 3, dc in next 3 dc, [ch 1, sk next ext st, dc in next 4 dc] across, turn.

Rows 13–20: Rep row 2, changing to B at end of row 20.

Row 21: Ch 3, dc in next 3 dc, [**ext st** *(see Special Stitches)* over next vertical row of ch-1 sps, dc in next 4 dc] across, turn.

Row 22: Ch 3, dc in next 3 dc, [ch 1, sk next ext st, dc in next 4 dc] across, turn.

Rows 23–30: Rep row 2, changing to A at end of row 30.

Rows 31–110: [Rep rows 21–30 consecutively] 8 times, changing colour at end of every 10th row. Change to A at end of row 110.

Row 111: Ch 3, dc in next 3 dc, *ext st over next vertical row of ch-1 sps, dc in next 4 dc, rep from * to last ch-1 sp, ext st over last vertical row of ch-1 sps, dc in next 3 dc, 3 dc in last dc, turn.

Border

Working along side of Afghan, 2 dc in end of each row to next corner, 3 dc in first st of foundation ch, dc in each st to last st of foundation ch, 3 dc in last st, 2 dc in end of each row to next corner, 2 dc in same st as beg ch-3 of row 111, sl st in top of beg ch-3.

Fasten off and weave in all ends. ◆

Warm Weavings

An alternating pattern of front and back post stitches creates a basket weave effect in this rustic throw.

DESIGN BY MARTY MILLER

Skill Level
■■□□
EASY

Finished Size
Approximately 44 x 54 inches

Materials
- Caron Simply Soft Tweed medium (worsted) weight yarn (3 oz/150 yds/85g per skein): 19 skeins #0007 autumn red
- Size I/9/5.5mm crochet hook or size needed to obtain gauge
- Tapestry needle

Gauge
14 sts = 4 inches; Square = 11 x 11 inches

Special Stitches
Back post double crochet (bpdc): Yo, insert hook from back to front to back around **post** (see Stitch Guide, p. 31) of st indicated, draw lp through, [yo, draw through 2 lps on hook] twice.

Front post double crochet (fpdc): Yo, insert hook from front to back to front around **post** (see Stitch Guide) of st indicated, draw lp through, [yo, draw through 2 lps on hook] twice.

Centre
Row 1 (RS): Ch 146; dc in 4th ch from hook *(beg 3 sk chs count as a dc)* and in each rem ch, turn. *(144 dc)*

Row 2: Ch 2 *(counts as a hdc on this and following rows)*, sk first dc; ***bpdc** (see Special Stitches) around each of next 4 dc, **fpdc** (see Special Stitches) around each of next 2 dc; rep from * to last 4 sts and beg 3 sk chs; bpdc around each of next 4 dc, hdc between last dc and beg 3 sk chs, turn.

Row 3: Ch 2, sk first hdc; *fpdc around each of next 4 sts, bpdc around each of next 2 sts; rep from * to last 4 sts and turning ch-2; fpdc around each of next 4 sts, hdc between last dc and turning ch-2, turn.

Row 4: Ch 2, sk first hdc; *bpdc around each of next 4 sts, fpdc around each of next 2 sts; rep from * to last 4 sts and turning ch-2; bpdc around each of next 4 sts, hdc between last dc and turning ch-2, turn.

Row 5: Ch 2, sk first dc; *bpdc around each of next 4 dc, fpdc around each of next 2 dc; rep from * to last 4 sts and turning ch-2; bpdc around each of next 4 dc, hdc between last dc and turning ch-2, turn.

Rows 6 & 7: Rep row 3.

Row 8: Rep row 5.

Row 9: Rep row 3.

Rows 10 & 11: Rep row 5.

Row 12: Rep row 3.

Rows 13–138: [Work rows 7–12 consecutively] 21 times.

Rows 139–142: Rep rows 7–10.

Border
Rnd 1 (RS): Ch 1, 3 sc in first hdc—*corner made*; sc in each st to turning ch-2; 3 sc in 2nd ch of turning ch—*corner made*; working across next side in ends of rows, sc evenly spaced to next corner; working across next side in unused lps of beg ch, 3 sc in first lp—*corner made*; sc in each lp to last lp; 3 sc in last lp—*corner made*; working across next side in ends of rows, sc evenly spaced to first sc; join with sl st in first sc.

Rnd 2: Ch 1, sc in same sc; 3 sc in next sc—*corner made*; *sc in each sc to 2nd sc of next corner; 3 sc in 2nd sc—*corner made*; rep from * twice; sc in each sc to first sc; join with sl st in first sc. Fasten off and weave in ends. ◆

Watermelon Print Throw

A simple pattern worked in a delicious blend of fruity colours gives tasteful style to this easy throw.

DESIGN BY KATHERINE ENG

Skill Level

EASY

Finished Size

44 x 66 inches

Materials

- Medium (worsted) weight yarn: 32 oz/1600 yds/907g pink multi, 6 oz/300 yds/170g pink
- Size K/10½/6.5mm crochet hook or size needed to obtain gauge
- Tapestry needle

Gauge

Rows 1 & 2 = 1¾ inches at points; 4 dc groups across = 4 inches

Pattern Note

Weave in loose ends as work progresses.

Throw

First Half

Row 1 (RS): Starting at centre with pink multi, ch 160, 2 dc in 4th ch from hook, [sk next 3 chs, (sl st, ch 3, 2 dc) in next ch] across to last 4 chs, sk next 3 chs, sc in last ch, turn. *(39 dc groups)*

Row 2: Ch 3 *(counts as first ch-3 sp of row)*, 2 dc in first sc, [(sl st, ch 3, 2 dc) in next ch-3 sp] across, ending with sc in last ch-3 sp, turn.

Rows 3–30: Rep row 2. At the end of row 30, fasten off.

Row 31 (RS): Attach pink in sc, ch 3, 2 dc in first sc, [(sl st, ch 3, 2 dc) in next ch-3 sp] across, ending with sc in last ch-3 sp, turn.

Rows 32–35: Rep row 2. At the end of row 35, fasten off.

Second Half

Row 1 (RS): With RS of First Half facing and working in opposite side of foundation ch, attach pink multi in first ch, ch 3, 2 dc in same ch as beg ch-3, [sk next 3 chs, (sl st, ch 3, 2 dc) in next ch] across to last 4 chs, sk next 3 chs, sc in last ch, turn. *(39 dc groups)*

Rows 2–30: Rep row 2 of First Half.

Rows 31–35: Rep rows 31–35 of First Half.

Border

Row 1 (RS): Working in side edge of rows, attach pink with sl st in side edge of end sc of row 35, ch 1, sc in same st as beg ch-1, [(sc, ch 3, sc) in side edge of each ch-3 sp, sc in end of each sc row] across entire edge of Throw, working a sc in centre foundation ch, fasten off.

Rep row 1 of Border on opposite side edge of rows of Throw. ✦

Bold Blocks Afghan

Eye-catching blocks of colour mingle with comfy bouclé yarn for a sophisticated-looking afghan.

DESIGN BY LOUISE PUCHATY

Skill Level

INTERMEDIATE

Finished Size

47 x 51 inches

Materials

- Bernat Soft Bouclé bulky weight yarn (5 oz/255 yds/140g per skein): 3 skeins #06756 black, 3 skeins each #06703 natural and #22011 soft taupe, 1 skein #26530 richest red
- Size J/10/6mm crochet hook or size needed to obtain gauge
- Yarn needle

Gauge

6 sc = 2 inches; 5 rows = 2 inches

Pattern Notes

Weave in loose ends as work progresses.

Afghan is crocheted vertically in 17 narrow panels and then sewn together.

Panel A

Make 5.

Row 1: With black, ch 9, sc in 2nd ch from hook, sc in each rem ch across, turn. *(8 sc)*

Rows 2–153: Ch 1, sc in each sc across, turn. At the end of row 153, fasten off.

Panel B

Make 8.

Row 1: With black, ch 9, sc in 2nd ch from hook, sc in each rem ch across, turn. *(8 sc)*

Row 2: Ch 1, sc in each sc across, turn.

Rows 3–9: Rep row 2. At the end of row 9, **change colour** *(see Stitch Guide, p. 31)* to soft taupe, turn.

Rows 10–36: Rep row 2. At the end of row 36, change colour to black, turn.

Rows 37–45: Rep row 2. At the end of row 45, change colour to natural, turn.

Rows 46–72: Rep row 2. At the end of row 72, change colour to black, turn.

Rows 73–81: Rep row 2. At the end of row 81, change colour to soft taupe, turn.

Rows 82–108: Rep row 2. At the end of row 108, change colour to black, turn.

Rows 109–117: Rep row 2. At the end of row 117, change colour to natural, turn.

Rows 118–144: Rep row 2. At the end of row 144, change colour to black, turn.

Row 145–153: Rep row 2. At the end of row 153, fasten off.

Panel C

Make 4.

Row 1: With black, ch 9, sc in 2nd ch from hook, sc in each rem ch across, turn. *(8 sc)*

Row 2: Ch 1, sc in each sc across, turn.

Rows 3–9: Rep row 2. At the end of row 9, change colour to soft taupe, turn.

Rows 10–18: Rep row 2. At the end of row 18, change colour to richest red, turn.

Rows 19–27: Rep row 2. At the end of row 27, change colour to soft taupe, turn.

Rows 28–36: Rep row 2. At the end of row 36, change colour to black, turn.

Rows 37–45: Rep row 2. At the end of row 45, change colour to natural, turn.

Rows 46–54: Rep row 2. At the end of row 54, change colour to richest red, turn.

Rows 55–63: Rep row 2. At the end of row 63, change colour to natural, turn.

Rows 64–72: Rep row 2. At the end of row 72, change colour to black, turn.

CONTINUED ON PAGE 153

Midnight Magic Throw

Plush, super-bulky chenille yarn gives this sumptuous throw velvety softness, and single crochet stitches worked in the back loops provides rich texture.

BY FRANCES HUGHES

Skill Level

◼☐☐☐
BEGINNER

Finished Size

50 x 60 inches

Materials

- Sirdar Wow! chenille super bulky (super chunky) weight yarn (3½ oz/63 yds/100g per skein): 19 skeins #762 blue indigo
- Size L/11/8mm crochet hook or size needed to obtain gauge
- Tapestry needle

Gauge

5 sc = 3 inches

Pattern Notes

Weave in loose ends as work progresses.

Join rounds with a slip stitch unless otherwise stated.

Throw

Row 1: Ch 86, sc in 2nd ch from hook, sc in each rem ch across, turn. *(85 sc)*

Row 2: Ch 1, working in **back lps** *(see Stitch Guide, p. 31)* only, sc in each st across, turn.

Rows 3–106: Rep row 2. At the end of row 106, **do not fasten off.**

Border

Rnd 1: Working down side edge of row, [ch 3, sk 1 row, sc in next row] across *(54 ch-3 lps)*, working across opposite side of foundation ch, [ch 3, sk next ch, sc in next ch] across *(44 ch-3 lps)*, working across side edge of rows, [ch 3, sk 1 row, sc in next row] across *(54 ch-3 lps)*, working across row 106, [ch 3, sk next sc, sc in next sc] across, ending with ch 1, hdc in beg sc to form last ch-3 lp *(44 ch-3 lps)*. *(196 ch-3 lps total)*

Rnd 2: Ch 1, sc in same sp as beg ch-1, [ch 3, sc in next ch-3 sp] around, ending with ch 1, hdc in beg sc to form last ch-3 lp.

Rnd 3: Rep rnd 2, fasten off. ✦

Woodland Throw

Rich brown and earthy neutrals give rustic style to this cozy throw that's perfect for a library or den.

DESIGN BY DORA OHRENSTEIN

Skill Level

BEGINNER

Finished Size
39 x 41 inches

Materials
- Moda Dea Metro bulky (chunky) weight yarn (3½ oz/124 yds/100g per ball): 5 balls #9863 mocha latte *(A)*, 3 balls #9340 chocolate *(B)*
- Size I/9/5.5mm crochet hook or size needed to obtain gauge
- Tapestry needle

Gauge
5 hdc = 2 inches; 4 hdc rows = 2 inches

Pattern Notes
Weave in loose ends as work progresses.

Join rounds with a slip stitch unless otherwise stated.

Throw
Row 1: Starting at bottom with A, ch 106, hdc in 3rd ch from

hook *(2 sk chs count as first hdc)*, hdc in each rem ch across, turn. *(105 hdc)*

Row 2: Ch 2 *(counts as first hdc)*, hdc in each hdc across, turn.

Row 3: Ch 2, hdc in each hdc across, **change colour** *(see Stitch Guide, p. 31)* to B, turn.

Row 4: Ch 2, hdc in each hdc across, change colour to A, turn.

Rows 5 & 6: Rep row 2.

Row 7: Rep row 3.

Rows 8–75: [Rep rows 4–7 consecutively] 17 times. At the end of row 75, change colour to B, fasten off A.

Border
Rnd 76: With B, ch 1, sc in each st evenly spaced around outer edge of Throw, working 3 sc in each corner, join in beg sc.

Rnd 77: Ch 1, sc in each sc around, working 3 sc in centre corner sc of each corner, join in beg sc, fasten off. ✦

Bouclé Afghan

Autumn's colour palette is represented here in all its vivid glory. This beginner pattern features a bouclé yarn.

DESIGN BY KATHERINE ENG

Skill Level

EASY

Finished Size
41 x 62 inches

Materials
- Bulky (chunky) weight yarn: 22 oz/1706 yds/ 624g variegated brown (A)
- Jo-Ann Sensations Angel Hair bulky (chunky) weight yarn (3½ oz/120 yds/100g per skein): 2 skeins #201 berry (B)
- Size I/9/5.5mm crochet hook or size needed to obtain gauge
- Tapestry needle

Gauge
Rows 1–4 = 2 inches; 3 sc and 2 ch-2 sps across = 2 inches

Pattern Notes
Weave in loose ends as work progresses.

Join rounds with a slip stitch unless otherwise stated.

Afghan is crocheted from centre outward for first half and from foundation chain of first half at centre outward for 2nd half.

Row 1 establishes right side of afghan, turn at the end of each row.

Special Stitches
Shell: (2 dc, ch 2, 2 dc) in indicated st.
V-stitch (V-st): (Dc, ch 3, dc) in indicated st.

First Half
Row 1 (RS): With A, ch 182, sc in 2nd ch from hook, [ch 2, sk next 2 chs, sc in next ch] across, turn. *(61 sc, 60 ch-2 sps)*

Row 2: Ch 1, sc in first sc, [sk next ch-2 sp, **shell** *(see Special Stitches)* in next sc, sk next ch-2 sp, sc in next sc] across, turn. *(31 sc, 30 shells)*

Row 3: Ch 5 *(counts as first dc, ch 2)*, sc in next ch-2 sp, *ch 2, dc in next sc**, ch 2, sc in next ch-2 sp, rep from * across, ending last rep at **, turn. *(61 sts, 60 ch-2 sps)*

Row 4: Ch 1, sc in first dc, *ch 2, sk next ch-2 sp, sc in next sc, ch 2, sk next ch-2 sp, sc in next dc, rep from * across, ending last rep with ch 2, sk next 2 chs, sc in 3rd ch of ch-5, fasten off, turn.

Row 5: Draw up a lp of B in first sc, ch 1, sc in same sc as beg ch-1, *sk next ch-2 sp, **V-st** *(see Special Stitches)* in next sc, sk next ch-2 sp, sc in next sc, rep from * across, fasten off, turn. *(31 sc, 30 V-sts)*

Row 6: Draw up a lp of A in first sc, rep row 3.

Row 7: Rep row 4, **do not fasten off**, turn.

Row 8: Rep row 2.
Rows 9 & 10: Rep rows 3 and 4.
Rows 11–13: Rep rows 2–4. At the end of row 13, fasten off.
Rows 14–40: [Rep rows 5–13 consecutively] 3 times. At the end of row 40, fasten off.

Second Half
Row 1 (RS): Draw up a lp of A in first ch of opposite side of foundation ch of First Half, ch 1, sc in same ch as beg ch-1, [ch 2, sk 2 chs, sc in next ch] across, turn. *(61 sc, 60 ch-2 sps)*

Rows 2–40: Rep rows 2–40 of First Half.

Border
Notes: *Work rnd 1 in specified sc sts at end of rows and in ch-3 sps or posts of dc sts at end of every 3rd row. Work rnds 2 and 3 in specified sts and sps only, sk rem sts.*

Rnd 1 (RS): Draw up a lp of B in foundation ch at centre top, ch 1, sc in same ch as beg ch-1, *sk next 2 sc, V-st in next ch-3 sp, [sc in next sc, sk next sc, V-st in next ch-3 sp] across to corner ending with sk next sc, (sc, ch 3, sc) in next corner sc, working across side, [sk next ch-2 sp, V-st in next

CONTINUED ON PAGE 153

Spirals to Surround You

Contrasting blocks of stripes and swirls create perfect harmony in this striking pattern.

DESIGN BY LISA PFLUG

Skill Level

EASY

Finished Size

Approximately 46 x 67 inches

Materials

- Lion Brand Homespun bulky (chunky) weight yarn (6 oz/185 yd/170g per skein): 7 skeins #322 baroque (A)
- Lion Brand Suede bulky (chunky) weight yarn (3 oz/122 yds/85g per ball): 2 balls each #147 eggplant (B) and #146 fuchsia (C)
- Size J/10/6mm crochet hook or size needed to obtain gauge
- Stitch markers
- Tapestry needle

Gauge

9 dc = 4 inches

Spiral Motif
Make 12.

With A, ch 4, sl st to form a ring.
Note: *Rnds 1–5 are worked in continuous rnds. Do not join; mark beg of rnds.*
Rnd 1 (RS): In ring, work (sc, 2 hdc, 9 dc). *(12 sts)*
Rnd 2: Working in **back lps** *(see Stitch Guide, p. 31)* only, 2 dc in next sc, 2 dc in each rem st. *(24 sts)*
Rnd 3: Working in back lps only, 2 dc in next dc, dc in next st, [2 dc in next st, dc in next st] around. *(36 sts)*
Rnd 4: Working in back lps only, 2 dc in next dc, dc in next 2 sts, [2 dc in next st, dc in next 2 sts] around. *(48 sts)*
Rnd 5: Working in back lps only, 2 dc in next dc, dc in next 3 sts, [2 dc in next st, dc in next 3 sts] around, join with sl st in first dc. Fasten off. *(60 sts)*

Rnd 6: Hold Motif with last st at bottom, join B with sl st to **front lp** *(see Stitch Guide, p. 31)* of last st, working in front lps only and from outside of Motif toward centre, sl st loosely in front lps until reaching centre.
Fasten off and pull loose end through centre of Motif.
Note: *For each Motif, join yarn on following rnd at a different point of spiral so they are oriented randomly.*
Rnd 7: With RS facing, join A with sc to back lp of any st on row 5, sc each st around, join with sl st in first sc.
Rnd 8: *Sc in next 2 sts, hdc in next 2 sts, dc in next 2 sts, tr in next st, 5 tr in next st—*corner made,* tr in next st, dc in next 2 sts, hdc in next 2 sts, sc in next 2 st, rep from * 3 times, join.
Rnd 9: Ch 3, *dc in each st to 3rd dc of next corner, 5 dc in 3rd dc, rep from * 3 times, dc in each st across, join with sl st in top of beg ch-3.
Fasten off and weave in all ends.

Stripe Motif
Make 12.

Row 1: With A, ch 26, dc in 4th ch from hook and in each ch across, turn. *(24 dc)*
Row 2: Ch 3 *(counts as a dc now and throughout)*, dc in each st across, turn. Fasten off.
Row 3: Join C with a sc in first st, sc in each st across, turn.
Row 4: Ch 1, sc in each st across, turn. Fasten off.
Row 5: Join A with sl st in first st, ch 3, dc in each st across, turn.
Row 6: Ch 3, dc in each st across, turn. Fasten off.

Row 7: Join B with a sc in first st, sc in each st across, turn. Fasten off.
Row 8: Join C with a sc in first st, sc in each st across, turn.
Row 9: Ch 1, sc in each st across, turn.
Rows 10 & 11: Rep row 9. Fasten off.
Row 12: Rep row 7.
Rows 13 & 14: Rep rows 5 and 6.
Rows 15–18: Rep rows 3–6. Fasten off and weave in all ends.

Assembly
Referring to diagram for placement of motifs and with A, sew motifs tog in 6 rows of 4 motifs each.

Edging
Row 1: With RS facing, join A with sl st to any corner, ch 3, 4 dc in same sp, *dc in each st to next corner, 5 dc in corner, rep from * twice more, dc in each st across, join with sl st in top of ch-3. Fasten off.
Row 2: With RS facing, join B with a sc to 3rd dc of any corner, 2 sc in same st, *sc in each st to 3rd dc of next corner, 3 sc in 3rd dc, rep from * twice more, sc in each st across, join with sl st in first sc.
Fasten off and weave in all ends. ◆

Spirals to Surround You

Sun-Washed Tiles

Cheerful blue and yellow tiles create a splash of sunny colour to accent a garden room or porch, or brighten any room in the home.

DESIGN BY KATHERINE ENG

Skill Level

INTERMEDIATE

Size
42 x 64 inches

Materials
- Lion Brand Homespun bulky (chunky) weight yarn (6 oz/185 yds/170g per skein): 4 skeins #355 delft and #372 sunshine state
- Size H/8/5mm crochet hook or size needed to obtain gauge
- Yarn needle

Gauge
Rnd 1 = 2½ inches; completed square = 5 inches
Check gauge to save time.

Pattern Notes
Weave in loose ends as work progresses.

Join rounds with a slip stitch unless otherwise stated.

Make 70 squares with colour combo 1 and 54 squares with alternate colour combo in parentheses.

Work all squares through rnd 2, weave in and sew down ends on wrong side, then join together as specified while working rnd 3.

Join in diagonal rows of alternate colour patterns beginning with sunshine state centre. Working diagonally, join seven squares in first row, six in following row, continue to alternate.

Special Stitch
Long double crochet (ldc): Yo, insert hook in indicated st, yo, draw up a lp, [yo, draw through 2 lps on hook] twice.

Square

Note: *Make 124 squares as indicated in Pattern Notes.*

Rnd 1 (RS): With sunshine state (delft), ch 4, sl st to join to form a ring, ch 3 *(counts as first dc throughout)*, 2 dc in ring, ch 2, [3 dc in ring, ch 2] 3 times, join in 3rd ch of beg ch-3, fasten off.

Rnd 2: Draw up a lp of delft (sunshine state) in any ch-2 sp, ch 3, (2 dc, ch 2, 3 dc) in same sp, ch 1, [(3 dc, ch 2, 3 dc) in next ch-2 sp, ch 1] 3 times, join in 3rd ch of beg ch-3, fasten off.

Rnd 3: Draw up a lp of sunshine state (delft) in 2nd dc to the left of any corner, ch 1, (sc, ch 2, sc) in same dc, *sk next dc, (**ldc**—*see Special Stitch, p. 49*, ch 2, ldc) over ch-1 sp in centre dc of rnd 1 directly below, sk next dc, (sc, ch 2, sc) in next dc, sk next dc, (sc, ch 4, sc) in corner ch-2 sp, sk next dc ******, (sc, ch 2, sc) in next dc, rep from * around, ending last rep at ******, join in beg sc, fasten off.

Assembly

Join squares tog on one or two sides as necessary. Continuing in pattern st of rnd 3, join corner ch-4 sps by ch 2, drop lp, draw lp under to over through opposite ch-4 sp, ch 2 and continue. To join ch-2 sps, ch 1, drop lp, draw lp under to over through opposite ch-2 sp, ch 1 and continue. To join where four corners meet, ch 2, drop lp, draw lp under to over through opposite ch-4 sp, ch 1, drop lp, sk next ch-4 sp, draw lp under to over through next ch-4 sp, ch 2, continue.

Border

Rnd 1 (RS): Draw up a lp of Inca in first ch-2 sp to the left of corner ch-4 sp on right-hand edge of square on long side but not at corner square, ch 1, *(sc, ch 2, sc) in first 3 ch-2 sp, [(sc, ch 2) 3 times and sc] in corner ch-4 sp ******, (sc, ch 2, sc) in each of next 3 ch-2 sps, working between seams, sc in next corner ch-4 sp, ch 2, sc in side of same sc, sk next *(centre)* ch-4 sp, sc in next ch-4 sp *, rep from * to * around working at each corner square, rep from * to ****** twice, (sc, ch 2, sc) in each of next 3 ch-2 sps and then work pattern for between seams, join in beg sc, fasten off. ◆

Patchwork Quilt Afghan

What a bright and cheerful quilt-look afghan! It consists of 19 panels, crocheted from bottom to top. So easy!

DESIGN BY LOUISE PUCHATY

Skill Level
■□□□
BEGINNER

Finished Size
63 x 63 inches

Materials
- Caron Simply Soft medium (worsted) weight yarn (6 oz/330 yds/170g per skein): 7 skeins #9701 white
- Caron Simply Soft Brites medium (worsted) weight yarn (6 oz/315 yds/170g per skein): 4 skeins #9608 blue mint, 3 skeins #9607 limelight, 2 skeins #9606 lemonade
- Size I/9/5.5mm crochet hook or size needed to obtain gauge
- Yarn needle

Gauge
Sc [ch 1, sk next st, sc] twice = 1 inch

Pattern Notes
Weave in loose ends as work progresses.

Join rounds with a slip stitch unless otherwise stated.

Afghan is made up of 19 panels crocheted from the bottom to top.

Sew panels together as each panel is completed.

Make 2 each of panels 1–9 and 1 of panel 10.

Afghan

Panel 1
Make 2.
Row 1: With white, ch 16, sc in 2nd ch from hook, [ch 1, sk next ch, sc in next ch] 7 times, turn. *(8 sc, 7 ch-1 sps)*
Row 2: Ch 1, sc in first sc, [ch 1, sk next ch-1 sp, sc in next sc] 7 times, turn.
Rows 3–266: Rep row 2. At the end of row 266, fasten off.

Panel 2
Make 2.
Row 1: With white, ch 16, sc in 2nd ch from hook, [ch 1, sk next ch, sc in next ch] 7 times, turn. *(8 sc, 7 ch-1 sps)*
Row 2: Ch 1, sc in first sc, [ch 1, sk next ch-1 sp, sc in next sc] 7 times, turn.
Rows 3–14: Rep row 2. At the end of row 14, **change colour** *(see Stitch Guide, p. 31)* to lemonade, turn.
Row 15: Ch 1, working in **back lp** *(see Stitch Guide)* of each st, sc in first st, [ch 1, sk next ch-1 sp, sc in next st] 7 times, turn.
Rows 16–28: Rep row 2. At the end of row 28, change colour to limelight, turn.
Row 29: Rep row 15.
Rows 30–42: Rep row 2. At the end of row 42, change colour to blue mint, turn.
Row 43: Rep row 15.
Rows 44–56: Rep row 2. At the end of row 56, change colour to white, turn.
Row 57: Rep row 15.
Rows 58–70: Rep row 2. At the end of row 70, change colour to lemonade, turn.
Row 71: Rep row 15.
Rows 72–84: Rep row 2. At the end of row 84, change colour to limelight, turn.
Row 85: Rep row 15.
Rows 86–98: Rep row 2. At the end of row 98, change colour to blue mint, turn.
Row 99: Rep row 15.
Rows 100–112: Rep row 2. At the end of row 112, change colour to white, turn.
Row 113: Rep row 15.
Rows 114–126: Rep row 2.
Row 127: Rep row 15.
Rows 128–140: Rep row 2.

Row 141: Rep row 15.

Rows 142–154: Rep row 2.

Row 155: Rep Row 15.

Rows 156–168: Rep row 2. At the end of row 168, change colour to blue mint, turn.

Row 169: Rep row 15.

Rows 170–182: Rep row 2. At the end of row 182, change colour to lemonade, turn.

Row 183: Rep row 15.

Rows 184–196: Rep row 2. At the end of Row 196, change colour white, turn.

Row 197: Rep row 15.

Rows 198–210: Rep row 2. At the end of row 210, change colour to blue mint, turn.

Row 211: Rep row 15.

Rows 212–224: Rep row 2. At the end of 224, change colour to limelight, turn.

Row 225: Rep row 15.

Row 226–238: Rep row 2. At the end of row 238, change colour to lemonade, turn.

Row 239: Rep row 15.

Rows 240–252: Rep row 2. At the end of row 252, change colour to white, turn.

Row 253: Rep row 15.

Rows 254–266: Rep row 2. At the end of row 266, fasten off.

Rem Panels

Using diagram of Patchwork Quilt afghan as a guide for colour sequence, continue to rep the same as Panels 1 and 2, changing colour as indicated.

Edging

Rnd 1: Attach white in any sc on outer edge, ch 1, sc evenly spaced around outer edge, working 3 sc in each corner st, join in beg sc, fasten off.

Rnd 2: Attach blue mint in any sc of rnd 1, ch 1, sc in each sc around working 3 sc in each centre corner sc, join in beg sc, fasten off. ◆

COLOUR KEY
☐ White
■ Blue mint
■ Limelight
☐ Lemonade

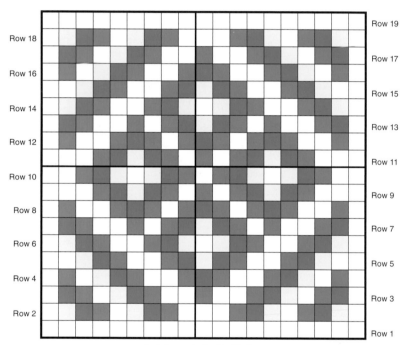

Patchwork Quilt Afghan

Squiggles & Giggles

Neon-bright colours dance in vivid stripes on a midnight-black background in this delightfully fun kid's afghan, highlighted with playful curlicues and ball fringe on each corner.

DESIGN BY RUTHIE MARKS

Skill Level

BEGINNER

Size

40 x 45 inches

Materials

- Medium (worsted) weight yarn: 30 oz/ 1650 yds/840g black, 5 oz/ 275 yds/140g each bright yellow, hot orange, hot lime, hot blue and hot pink
- Sizes G/6/4mm, I/9/5.5mm and J/10/6mm crochet hooks or size needed to obtain gauge
- Tapestry needle

Gauge

Size J hook: 6 dc = 2 inches; 3 rows = 2 inches
Check gauge to save time.

Pattern Notes

Weave in loose ends as work progresses.

Join rounds with a slip stitch unless otherwise stated.

Afghan

Row 1 (WS): With size J hook and black, ch 115, dc in 4th ch from hook, dc in each rem ch across, turn. *(113 dc)*
Row 2 (RS): Ch 2 *(counts as first dc throughout)*, working in **back lps** *(see Stitch Guide, p. 31)* only, dc in each st across, turn. *(113 dc)*
Row 3 (WS): Ch 2, working in both lps, dc in each dc across, turn. *(113 dc)*
Rep rows 2 and 3 until there are 35 rows worked in back lps only, ending with a row 2, **do not fasten off, do not turn.**

Edging

Rnd 1 (RS): Change to size I hook, ch 1, sc evenly spaced around, working 3 sc in each corner, join in beg sc, fasten off, turn.

Rounded Corners
Make 4.

Rnd 2 (WS): With size I hook, attach black with sl st in st before 3 centre corner sc sts, ch 1, 2 sc in first sc of corner, sc in middle sc of corner, 2 sc in last sc of corner, sl st in next st, fasten off.

Embellishments

Embellishments are worked in rem free lps of rows. Cut two pieces each 3 inches long of each colour, except black, for markers. Starting at row 1 of afghan, attach hot blue in rem free lp of row 4, hot pink in side edge of row 6, bright yellow in side edge of row 8, hot orange in side edge of row 10 and hot lime in side edge of row 12. Turn afghan so that last row is facing, beg with last row, count this as row 1 and rep attaching yarn colours the same as opposite end. Leave two sts unworked at beg and end of each row of embellishments.

Hot Blue
With size J hook, attach hot blue with sl st, ch 2 *(counts as first hdc)*, 3 hdc in same st, [4 hdc in next st] across, fasten off.

Hot Pink
With size J hook, attach hot pink, ch 1, sc in same st, [sk next st, 5 dc in next st, sk next st, sc in next st] across, fasten off.

Bright Yellow
With hook size J, attach bright yellow, ch 1, sc in same st, [ch 6, dc in top of sc, sk next 2 sts, sc in next st] across, fasten off.

Hot Orange
With size J hook, attach hot orange, ch 1, sc in same st, sc in each of next 3 sts, [4 dc in next st, draw up a lp, remove hook, insert hook back to front in first dc of 4-dc group, pick up dropped lp, draw through st on hook, ch 1, sc in each of next 3 sts] across, fasten off.

Hot Lime
Row 1: With size J hook, attach hot lime with sl st, ch 3, [yo, insert hook in same st, yo, draw up a lp, yo, draw through 2 lps on hook] twice, yo, draw through all 3 lps on hook, *ch 2, sk next 2 sts, [yo, insert hook in next st, yo, draw up a lp, yo, draw through 2 lps on hook] 3 times in same st, yo, draw through all 4 lps on hook, rep from * across, turn.
Row 2: Ch 1, sc in top of 3-dc group, [2 sc in next ch-2 sp, sc in top of 3-dc group] across, fasten off.

Corner Spirals
Make 1 each hot pink and hot orange; 2 each hot lime and bright yellow.
Note: Make spirals variously as desired in short, medium, and long lengths.
With size G hook, leaving an 8-inch length at beg, ch 20 [30, 35], working in top lps only, 2 sc in 2nd ch from hook, [2 sc in next ch] 13 [18, 18] times, leaving rem chs unworked, leaving a 4-inch length of yarn, fasten off. Thread 4-inch tail onto tapestry needle and secure top of spiral; trim rem length.

Corner Rosettes
Make 1 each hot pink and hot orange; 2 each hot lime and bright yellow.
Note: Make rosettes variously as desired in various small, medium and large sizes.
With size G hook, leaving an 8-inch length of yarn, ch 15 [20, 30], working in top lps, 3 dc in 4th ch from hook, *4 dc in next ch, rep from * in next 2 [3, 4] chs, leaving a 4-inch length, fasten off leaving rem 9 [13, 22] ch rem, thread tail into tapestry needle, shape flower and tack in place to secure.

Finishing
Gather tog 3 of the spirals or rosettes in 3 different colours and sizes, thread through tapestry needle, insert from front to back in centre st of rounded corner, secure in place with an overhand knot. Braid ends for approximately 3 inches, secure with another overhand knot, trim ends evenly, rep in each rem corner of afghan. ◆

Puffy Flowers Throw

Delightfully dimensional puff stitches create the plush flowers that dot this lacy romantic throw.

DESIGN BY NANCY NEHRING

Skill Level

EASY

Finished Size
45 x 55 inches

Materials
- Lion Brand Romance super bulky (super chunky) weight yarn (8 oz/480 yds/224g per ball): 2 balls #100 snowdrop
- Size P/15/10mm crochet hook or size needed to obtain gauge
- Tapestry needle

SUPER BULKY 6

Gauge
4 sc = 3 inches; 4 sc rows = 3 inches

Pattern Note
Weave in loose ends as work progresses.

Special Stitches
Beginning puff stitch (beg puff st): Ch 1, insert hook in next sc, yo, draw up a lp, [yo, insert hook in same sc, yo, draw up a lp] 3 times (8 lps on hook), sk next sc, insert hook in next sc, yo, draw up a lp, [yo, insert hook in same sc, yo, draw up a lp] 3 times, yo, draw through all 13 lps on hook, ch 1 to lock.

Ending puff stitch (ending puff st): Sk ch-1 locking st, insert hook in top of puff st of previous row, yo, draw up a lp, [yo, insert hook in same puff st of previous row, yo, draw up a lp] 3 times, yo, draw through all 8 lps on hook, ch 1 to lock, ch 1, insert hook in same puff st of previous row, yo, draw up a lp, [yo, insert hook in same puff st of previous row, yo, draw up a lp] 3 times, yo, draw through all 8 lps on hook, ch 1 to lock, sk next ch-1.

Throw
Row 1: Starting at bottom edge, ch 64, sc in 2nd ch from hook, sc in each rem ch across, turn. (63 sc)

Row 2: Ch 1, sc in each sc across, turn.

Row 3: Rep row 2.

Row 4: Ch 1, sc in each of next 2 sc, [work **beg puff st** (see Special Stitches), sc in each of next 5 sc] 7 times, work beg puff st, sc in each of next 2 sc, turn. (8 beg puff sts, 39 sc)

Row 5: Ch 1, sc in each of next 2 sc, [work **ending puff st** (see Special Stitches), sc in each of next 5 sc] 7 times, work ending puff st, sc in each of next 2 sc,

turn. (8 ending puff sts, 39 sc)

Row 6: Ch 1, sc in each of next 2 sc, [sc in top of puff st, sc in ch-1 sp between puff sts, sc in top of next puff st, sc in each of next 5 sc] 7 times, sc in top of next puff st, sc in ch-1 sp between puff sts, sc in top of next puff st, sc in each of next 2 sc, turn. (63 sc)

Rows 7–10: Rep row 2.

Row 11: Ch 1, sc in each of next 6 sc, [beg puff st, sc in each of next 5 sc] 7 times, sc in last sc, turn.

Row 12: Ch 1, sc in each of next 6 sc, [ending puff st, sc in each of next 5 sc] 7 times, sc in last sc, turn.

Row 13: Ch 1, sc in each of next 6 sc, [sc in top of next puff st, sc in ch-1 sp between puff sts, sc in top of next puff st, sc in each of next 5 sc] 7 times, sc in next sc, turn. (63 sc)

Rows 14–17: Rep row 2.

Rows 18–73: [Rep rows 4–17 consecutively] 4 times.

Row 74–78: Rep rows 4–8. ◆

Gramma & Grandbabies

Granny squares both large and small make this traditional favourite easy and fun to stitch.

DESIGN BY MARTY MILLER

Skill Level
◼◼◻◻
EASY

Finished Size
Approximately 56 x 64 inches

Materials
- Plymouth Encore medium (worsted) weight yarn (3½ oz/200 yds/100g per ball): 4 balls each #2764 champagne (A) and #175 jewel gold (B), 3 skeins each #180 dark mauve (C) and #45 English fern (D)
- Size I/9/5.5mm crochet hook or size needed to obtain gauge
- Tapestry needle

Gauge
Rnds 1–4 = 5½ inches in diameter

Centre
Large Square
Rnd 1 (RS): With C, ch 4; join with sl st to form ring; ch 3 *(counts as a dc on this and following rnds)*, 2 dc in ring; ch 1, [3 dc in ring, ch 1] 3 times; join with sl st in 3rd ch of beg ch-3. *(12 dc)*
Rnd 2: Sl st in next 2 dc and in next ch-1 sp; ch 3, in same sp work (2 dc, ch 1, 3 dc)—*beg corner made*; ch 1; *in next ch-1 sp work (3 dc, ch 1, 3 dc)—*corner made*; ch 1; rep from * twice; join with sl st in 3rd ch of beg ch-3.
Rnd 3: Sl st in next 2 dc and in next ch-1 sp; beg corner in same sp; 3 dc in next ch-1 sp; ch 1; *in next corner ch-1 sp work corner; ch 1, 3 dc in next ch-1 sp, ch 1; rep from * twice; join with sl st in 3rd ch of beg ch-3.
Rnd 4: Sl st in next 2 dc and in next ch-1 sp; beg corner in same sp; ch 1, [3 dc in next ch-1 sp, ch 1] twice; *corner in next corner ch-1 sp; ch 1, [3 dc in next ch-1 sp, ch 1] twice; rep from * twice; join with sl st in the 3rd ch of beg ch-3. Fasten off.
Rnd 5: Join D with sl st in ch-1 sp of any corner; beg corner in same sp; ch 1, [3 dc in next ch-1 sp, ch 1] 3 times; *corner in next corner ch-1 sp; ch 1, [3 dc in next ch-1 sp, ch 1] 3 times; rep from * twice; join with sl st in the 3rd ch of beg ch-3.
Rnd 6: Sl st in next 2 dc and in next ch-1 sp; beg corner in same sp; ch 1, [3 dc in next ch-1 sp, ch 1] 4 times; *corner in next corner ch-1 sp; ch 1, [3 dc in next ch-1 sp, ch 1] 4 times; rep from * twice; join with sl st in the 3rd ch of beg ch-3.
Rnd 7: Sl st in next 2 dc and in next ch-1 sp; beg corner in same sp; ch 1, [3 dc in next ch-1 sp, ch 1] 5 times; *corner in next corner ch-1 sp; ch 1, [3 dc in next ch-1 sp, ch 1] 5 times; rep from * twice; join with sl st in the 3rd ch of beg ch-3. Fasten off.
Rnd 8: Join A with sl st in ch-1 sp of any corner; beg corner in same sp; ch 1, [3 dc in next ch-1 sp, ch 1] 6 times; *corner in next corner ch-1 sp; ch 1, [3 dc in next ch-1 sp, ch 1] 6 times; rep from * twice; join with sl st in the 3rd ch of beg ch-3.
Rnd 9: Sl st in next 2 dc and in next ch-1 sp; beg corner in same sp; ch 1, [3 dc in next ch-1 sp, ch 1] 7 times; *corner in next corner ch-1 sp; ch 1, [3 dc in next ch-1 sp, ch 1] 7 times; rep from * twice; join with sl st in the 3rd ch of beg ch-3. Fasten off.
Rnd 10: Join B with sl st in ch-1 sp of any corner; beg corner in same sp; *ch 1, in each ch-1 sp to next corner work (3 dc, ch 1); corner in next corner ch-1 sp; rep from * twice; ch 1, in each rem ch-1 sp work (3 dc, ch 1); join with sl st in the 3rd ch of beg ch-3.

Rnd 11: Sl st in next 2 dc and in next ch-1 sp; beg corner in same sp; *ch 1, in each ch-1 sp to next corner work (3 dc, ch 1); corner in next corner ch-1 sp; rep from * twice; ch 1, in each rem ch-1 sp work (3 dc, ch 1); join with sl st in the 3rd ch of beg ch-3.

Rnds 12 & 13: Rep rnd 11. Fasten off at end of rnd 13.

Rnd 14: With C, rep rnd 10.

Rnds 15 & 16: Rep rnd 11. Fasten off at end of rnd 16.

Rnd 17: With D, rep rnd 10.

Rnd 18: Rep rnd 11. Fasten off.

Rnd 19: With A, rep rnd 10.

Rnds 20–22: Rep rnd 11. Fasten off at end of rnd 22.

Rnd 23: With B, rep rnd 10.

Rnds 24 & 25: Rep rnd 11. Fasten off at end of rnd 25.

Rnd 26: With C, rep rnd 10.

Rnd 27: Rep rnd 11. Fasten off.

Rnd 28: With D, rep rnd 10.

Rnds 29–31: Rep rnd 11. Fasten off at end of rnd 31.

Rnd 32: With A, rep rnd 10.

Rnds 33 & 34: Rep rnd 11. Fasten off at end of rnd 34.

Rnd 35: With B, rep rnd 10.

Rnd 36: Rep rnd 11.
Fasten off and weave in all ends.

Small Square

Square A

Rnd 1 (RS): With B, ch 4; join with sl st to form ring; ch 3 *(counts as a dc on this and following rnds)*, 2 dc in ring; ch 1, [3 dc in ring, ch 1] 3 times; join with sl st in 3rd ch of beg ch-3. *(12 dc)* Fasten off.

Rnd 2: Join C with sl st in any ch-1 sp; ch 3, in same sp work (2 dc, ch 1, 3 dc)—*beg corner made*; ch 1; *in next ch-1 sp work (3 dc, ch 1, 3 dc)—*corner made*; ch 1; rep from * twice; join with sl st in 3rd ch of beg ch-3. Fasten off.

Rnd 3: Join D with sl st in ch-1 sp of any corner; beg corner in same sp; 3 dc in next ch-1 sp; ch 1; *in next corner ch-1 sp work corner; ch 1, 3 dc in next ch-1 sp, ch 1; rep from * twice; join with sl st in 3rd ch of beg ch-3. Fasten off.

Rnd 4: Join A with sl st in ch-1 sp of any corner; beg corner in same sp; ch 1, [3 dc in next ch-1 sp, ch 1] twice; *corner in next corner ch-1 sp; ch 1, [3 dc in next ch-1 sp, ch 1] twice; rep from * twice; join with sl st in the 3rd ch of beg ch-3. Fasten off.

Square B

With D, work same as rnds 1–4 of Large Square.

Square C

Work same as rnds 1–4 of Square A, working rnds in following colour sequence: A, B, A, B.

Square D

Work same as rnds 1–4 of Square A, working rnds in following colour sequence: C, C, D, D.

Square E

Work same as rnds 1–4 of Square A, working rnds in following colour sequence: B, C, B, C.

Square F

Work same as rnds 1–4 of Square A, working rnds in following colour sequence: D, D, A, A.

Square G

Work same as rnds 1–4 of Square A, working rnds in following colour sequence: D, B, D, B.

Square H

With C, work same as Square B.

Square I

Work same as rnds 1–4 of Square A, working rnds in following colour sequence: A, B, C, D.

Square J

Work same as rnds 1–4 of Square A, working rnds in following colour sequence: D, A, B, C.

Square K

With B, work same as Square B.

Square L

Work same as rnds 1–4 of Square A, working rnds in following colour sequence: D, A, D, A.

Square M

Work same as rnds 1–4 of Square A, working rnds in following colour sequence: B, B, C, C.

Square N

Work same as rnds 1–4 of Square A, working rnds in following colour sequence: C, A, C, A.

Square O

Work same as rnds 1–4 of Square A, working rnds in following colour sequence: A, A, B, B.

Square P

Work same as rnds 1–4 of Square A, working rnds in following colour sequence: C, D, C, D.

Square Q

With A, work same as Square B.

Square R

Work same as rnds 1–4 of Square A, working rnds in following colour sequence: C, D, A, B.

Assembly

Join Squares tog to form Top Strip and Bottom Strip as follows: Hold Square A and Square B with WS tog; with matching yarn and working in **back lps** *(see Stitch Guide, p. 31)* only, sew across 1 side, beg and ending in corner ch-1 sps. Referring to Top Strip diagram for placement, join Squares C–I in same

manner. Referring to Bottom Strip diagram for placement, sew Squares J–R tog in same manner.

Hold WS of Top Strip facing WS of 1 side of Centre Square. With B and working in back lps only, sew across side, beg and ending in ch-1 sps of outer corners. Sew Bottom Strip to opposite side of Centre Square in same manner.

Border

Rnd 1 (RS): Hold piece with RS facing you and Top Strip at top; join C with sl st in ch-1 sp in upper right-hand corner; ch 3 *(counts as a dc on this and following rnds)*, in same sp work (2 dc, ch 1, 3 dc)—*beg corner made*; *ch 1, in each ch-1 sp to next corner work (3 dc, ch 1); in corner ch-1 sp work (3 dc, ch 1, 3 dc, ch 1)—*corner made*; rep from * twice; ch 1, in each rem ch-1 sp work (3 dc, ch 1); join with sl st in 3rd ch of beg ch-3. Fasten off.

Rnd 2: Hold piece with RS facing you; join D with sl st in ch-1 sp in upper right-hand corner; beg corner in same sp; *ch 1, in each ch-1 sp to next corner work (3 dc, ch 1); in corner ch-1 sp work corner; rep from * twice; ch 1, in each rem ch-1 sp work (3 dc, ch 1); join

with sl st in 3rd ch of beg ch-3. Fasten off.

Rnds 3–8: Rep rnd 2 in following colour sequence: A, B, C, D, A, B.

Edging

Hold piece with RS facing you; join D with sl st in ch-1 sp in upper right-hand corner; ch 3 *(counts as a dc)*, 2 dc in same sp; ch 1; *sc in next ch-1 sp, ch 1, in next ch-1 sp work (3 dc, ch 1, 3 dc); ch 1; rep from * 24 times; sc in next ch-1 sp, ch 1, 3 dc in next corner ch-1 sp, ch 1; **change colour** to A by drawing lp through; cut D; 3 dc in same sp; **sc in next ch-1 sp, ch 1, in next ch-1 sp work (3 dc, ch 1, 3 dc); ch 1; rep from ** 25 times; sc in next ch-1 sp, ch 1, 3 dc in next corner ch-1 sp, ch 1; change to B by drawing lp through; cut A; 3 dc in same sp; ***sc in next ch-1 sp, ch 1, in next ch-1 sp work (3 dc, ch 1, 3 dc); ch 1; rep from *** 24 times; sc in next ch-1 sp, ch 1, 3 dc in next corner ch-1 sp, ch 1; change to C by drawing lp through; cut B; 3 dc in same sp; ****sc in next ch-1 sp, ch 1, in next ch-1 sp work (3 dc, ch 1, 3 dc); ch 1; rep from **** 25 times; sc in next ch-1 sp, ch 1, 3 dc in next corner ch-1 sp; ch 1; join with sl st in 3rd ch of beg ch-3.

Fasten off and weave in all ends. ◆

Top Strip Diagram

Bottom Strip Diagram

Gramma & Grandbabies

Warming Trend Versatile Afghan

Luxurious mohair yarn worked in a super-easy shell pattern makes this design an all-around winner.

DESIGN BY CINDY ADAMS

Skill Level

BEGINNER

Finished Size
Approximately 40 x 54 inches

Materials
- Wendy Paris Mohair medium (worsted) weight yarn (1 3/4 oz/109 yds/50g per ball): 9 balls #1255 horizon (B)
- Size J/10/6mm crochet hook or size needed to obtain gauge
- Tapestry needle

Gauge
4 shells = 5 inches

Special Stitch
Shell: In st or sp indicated work (sc, ch 3, 2 dc).

Afghan

Centre
Row 1: Ch 92, sc in 2nd ch from hook and in each ch across. (91 sc)
Row 2: Shell (see Special Stitch) in first sc, sk next 2 sc, [shell in next sc, sk next 2 sc] across to last sc, sc in last sc, turn. (30 shells)
Row 3: Ch 1, shell in first sc, [shell in ch-3 sp of next shell] to last shell, sc in ch-3 sp of last shell, turn.
Rep row 3 until piece measures 60 inches. At end of last row, **do not turn.**

Border
Work shells evenly spaced along side of Afghan, across lower edge in unused lps of beg ch and along next side of Afghan, join with sl st in sc of first shell of last row worked.
Fasten off and weave in all ends. ✦

Smoke & Mirrors Afghan

You'll love the sumptuous feel and easy style of this luscious, quick-to-stitch afghan.

DESIGN BY RENA V. STEVENS

Skill Level

INTERMEDIATE

Finished Size

40 x 55 inches, excluding fringe

Materials

- Lion Brand Jiffy or bulky (chunky) weight acrylic yarn (3 oz/135 yds/85g per ball): 5 balls #100 white *(A)* 2 skeins each #155 silver heather *(B)* and #150 pearl grey *(C)*
- Size P/15mm crochet hook or size needed to obtain gauge
- Tapestry needle

Gauge

9 sc = 5 inches

Pattern Notes

Afghan is worked vertically. When joining and fastening off yarn, leave an 8-inch length to be worked into fringe.

Special Stitches

Inverted V-st (inv V-st): Holding back on hook last lp of each st, dc in same st as last half of last inv V-st made, sk next st, dc in next st, yo, draw through all 3 lps on hook.

Beginning inverted V-st (beg inv V-st): Holding back on hook last lp of each st, dc in fourth ch from hook, sk next ch, dc in next ch, yo, draw through all 3 lps on hook.

Afghan

Row 1: With A, ch 106, **beg inv V-st** *(see Special Stitches)*, [ch 1, **inv V-st** *(see Special Stitches)*] rep across, ending with dc in same st as last half of last inv V-st. Fasten off. Turn. *(51 inv V-sts; 50 ch-1 sps; 1 dc at each end, counting last 3 chs of foundation ch as first dc)*

Row 2 (RS): Join B with a sl st in first dc, ch 1, sc in same dc, sc in each inv V-st and in each ch-1 sp across, ending with sc in last inv V-st, sc in next ch. Fasten off. Turn. *(103 sc)*

Row 3: Working in **front lps** only this row *(see Stitch Guide, p. 31)*, join C with a sl st in first sc, ch 1, sc in same sc, sc in each rem sc across. Fasten off. Turn.

Row 4: Join A with a sl st in first sc, ch 3 *(counts as first dc throughout)*; beg in same st as ch-3, inv V-st, [ch 1, inv V-st] rep across, ending with dc in same st as last half of last inv V-st. Fasten off. Turn. *(51 inv V-sts, 50 ch-1 sps, 1 dc at each end)*

Row 5: Join B with a sl st in first dc, ch 2 *(counts as first hdc throughout)*, hdc in each inv V-st and in each ch-1 sp across, ending with V-st in top of first ch-3. Fasten off. Turn. *(103 hdc)*

Row 6: Working in **back lps** only this row *(see Stitch Guide)*, join C with a sl st in first hdc, ch 2, hdc in each rem hdc across. Fasten off. Turn.

Row 7: Join A with a sl st in first hdc, rep row 4. Do not fasten off. Turn. *(51 inv V-sts, 50 ch-1 sps, 1 dc at each end)*

Row 8: Ch 3, beg in same st as ch-3, inv V-st, [ch 1, inv V-st] rep across, ending with dc in same st as last half of last inv V-st. Fasten off. Turn.

Row 9: With C, rep row 5.

Row 10: With B, rep row 6.

Row 11: Rep row 7. Fasten off. Turn.

Row 12: With C, rep row 2, ending with sc in last inv V-st, sc in top of ch-3. Fasten off. Turn

Row 13: With B, rep row 3.

CONTINUED ON PAGE 153

Wrap-Yourself-Up Lush Shawl

Plush, bulky yarn worked in an open stitch pattern makes this delicious wrap cozy, yet light as air.

DESIGN BY ZELDA WORKMAN

Skill Level

EASY

Finished Size

Approximately 27 x 87 inches

Materials

- Patons Divine bulky (chunky) weight yarn (3½ oz/142 yds/100g per ball): 6 balls #06740 floral fantasy

- Size M/13/9mm crochet hook or size needed to obtain gauge
- Tapestry needle
- Stitch marker

Gauge

6 V-sts = 9 inches

Special Stitch

V-stitch (V-st): In st or sp indicated work (dc, ch 1, dc).

Shawl

Row 1 (RS): Ch 47, sc in 2nd ch from hook and in each ch across, turn. *(46 sc)*

Row 2: Ch 3 *(counts as dc)*, sk first sc, dc in next sc, sk next sc, **V-st *(see Special Stitch)* in next sc, sk next 2 sc, rep from * to last 3 sc, sk next sc, dc in last 2 sc, turn. *(14 V-sts)*

Row 3: Ch 3, sk first dc, dc in next dc, **V-st in ch-1 sp of next V-st, rep from * to last 2 dc, dc in last 2 dc, turn. *(14 V-sts)*

Rep row 3 until piece measures approximately 78 inches, ending with a RS row, turn.

Next row (WS): Ch 1, sc in each st across, turn. *(46 sc)*

Do not fasten off.

Edging

Rnd 1 (RS): Ch 1, sc in first sc, [ch 3, sk next 2 sc, sc in next sc] across; working along next side in sps formed by edge st, [ch 3, sc in next sp] across; ch 3, working in unused lps of beg ch, sc in first lp [ch 3, sk next 2 lps, sc in next lp] across; working along next side in sps formed by edge st, [ch 3, sc in next sp] across, join with sl st in first sc.

Rnd 2: [Ch 3, sc in next ch-3 sp] around. **Do not join.** Mark last ch-3 sp.

Rnds 3–5: [Ch 3, sc in next ch-3 sp] around, marking last ch-3 sp on each rnd. At end of rnd 5, ch 3, sl st in marked ch-3 sp. Fasten off and weave in all ends. ◆

My Blue Denim Wrap Afghan

Cloud-soft yarn in chic, denim hues make this cozy afghan perfect for a dorm room.

DESIGN BY EDIE ECKMAN

Skill Level

EASY

Finished Size

Approximately 39 x 54 inches

Materials

- Patons Divine bulky (chunky) weight yarn (3½ oz/142 yds/100g per ball): 9 balls #06117 denim storm
- Size M/13/9mm crochet hook or size needed to obtain gauge
- Tapestry needle

Gauge

7 sts = 4 inches

Special Stitches

Back post double crochet (bpdc): Yo, insert hook from back to front around **post** (see Stitch Guide, p. 31) of next st, yo, draw lp through, [yo, draw through 2 lps on hook] twice.

Front post double crochet (fpdc): Yo, insert hook from front to back around **post** (see Stitch Guide) of next st, yo, draw lp through, [yo, draw through 2 lps on hook] twice.

Afghan

Row 1 (RS): Ch 76, dc in 3rd ch from hook and in each ch across, turn. (74 sts)

Row 2: Ch 2 (counts as a dc now and throughout), **fpdc** (see Special Stitches) around next 2 st, **bpdc** (see Special Stitches) around next st [fpdc around next 3 sts, bpdc around next st] across to last 3 sts, fpdc around next 2 sts, dc in 2nd ch of beg ch-2, turn.

Row 3: Ch 2, dc in next 2 sts, [fpdc around next st, dc in next 3 st] across, ending with a dc in 2nd ch of beg ch-2, turn.

Row 4: Ch 2, fpdc around next 2 sts, bpdc around next st, [fpdc around next 3 sts, bpdc around next st] across to last 3 sts, fpdc around next 2 sts, dc in 2nd ch of beg ch-2, turn.

Rep rows 3 and 4 until piece measures approximately 54 inches, ending with row 3. Fasten off and weave in all ends. ✦

Paris Stitch Captivating Capelet

Wear this versatile wrap fastened in the front or on the shoulder. It looks great either way!

DESIGN BY LAURA GEBHARDT

Skill Level

EASY

Finished Size

Approximately 36 x 19 inches

Materials

- Patons Bohemian super bulky (super chunky) weight yarn (2¾ oz/68 yds/80g per ball): 6 balls #11530 cranberry café
- Size K/10½/6.5mm crochet hook or size needed to obtain gauge
- Tapestry needle
- 1-inch diameter button
- Sewing needle and matching thread

Gauge

3 pattern reps = 4 inches; 5½ rows = 4 inches

Special Stitch

Paris stitch (Paris st): In st or sp indicated work (2 dc, ch 2, sc).

Capelet

Row 1 (RS): Ch 79, (dc, ch 2, sc) in 3rd ch from hook *(beg 2 sk chs count as a dc),* *sk next 2 chs, **Paris st** *(see Special Stitch)* in next ch; rep from * across, turn. *(26 pst)*

Row 2: Ch 3, (dc, ch 2, sc) in next ch-2 sp, pst in each ch-2 sp across, turn.

Rep row 2 until piece measures approximately 18 inches from beg. Fasten off.

Edging

Hold piece with RS of row 1 at top, join yarn in first ch-2 sp on row 1, ch 3, (dc, ch 2, sc) in same ch, *sk next 2 chs, pst in next ch, rep from * across.

Fasten off and weave in all ends.

Finishing

Sew button to top left corner. Use ch-2 sp at top right corner as buttonhole. ✦

Wrap-Sody in Blue Blanket Coat

Self-striping yarn and seamless construction make this cozy Blanket-style coat a snap to make. Wear it as a wrap, belt it or pin it with a pretty brooch—the choice is yours!

DESIGN BY LAURA GEBHARDT

Skill Level

◼◼◻◻

EASY

Finished Size

Instructions given fit small, changes for medium, large, X-large and 2X-large are in [ ].

Finished Garment Measurements

Bust: 45 inches *(small)* [48 inches *(medium)*, 53½ inches *(large)*, 60¾ inches *(X-large)*, 66½ inches *(2X-large)*]

Materials

- Bernat Masala bulky (chunky) weight yarn (3½ oz/155 yds/100g per ball): 10 [11, 12, 14, 16] balls #78114 tidal tones
- Size K/10½/6.5mm crochet hook or size needed to obtain gauge
- Tapestry needle

Gauge

11 dc = 5 inches; 7 dc rows = 5 inches
Check gauge to save time.

Pattern Notes

Chain-2 at beginning of every row gives a neater edge than chain-3 and eliminates the need for an edging.

Chain-2 at the beginning of double crochet row or round is counted as first double crochet unless otherwise stated.

Coat is worked from side to side.

Coat

Row 1: Ch 119, dc in 3rd ch from hook *(first 2 chs count as first dc)* and in each ch across, turn. *(118 dc)*

Row 2: Ch 2 *(see Pattern Notes)*, dc in same st, dc in each st across, turn. *(119 dc)*

Row 3: Ch 2, dc in each st across with 2 dc in last st, turn. *(120 dc)*

Rows 4–11: [Rep rows 2 and 3 alternately] 4 times. *(128 dc at end of last row)*

Row 12: Rep row 2. *(129 dc)*

Rows 13–19 [13–19, 13–23, 13–27, 13–29]: Ch 2, dc in each st across, turn.

Row 20 [20, 24, 28, 30]: Ch 2, dc in each of next 32 sts, ch 22, sk next 22 sts *(armhole)*, dc in each st across, turn.

Row 21 [21, 25, 29, 31]: Ch 2, dc in each st and in each ch across, turn. *(129 dc)*

Rows 22–43 [22–47, 26–51, 30–57, 32–63]: Ch 2, dc in each st across, turn.

Row 44 [48, 52, 58, 64]: Ch 2, dc in each of next 32 sts, ch 22, sk next 22 sts *(armhole)*, dc in each st across, turn.

Row 45 [49, 53, 59, 65]: Ch 2, dc in each st and in each ch across, turn. *(129 dc)*

Rows 46–51 [50–55, 54–63, 60–73, 66–81]: Ch 2, dc in each st across, turn.

Row 52 [56, 64, 74, 82]: Ch 1, **dc dec** *(see Stitch Guide, p. 31)* in first 2 sts, dc in each st across, turn. *(128 dc)*

CONTINUED ON PAGE 154

Summer Waves Wrap

Makes "waves" in style with the vibrant ripple design in this soft, cotton wrap stitched in a mix of blues and greens.

DESIGN BY LYNNE WARDROP

Skill Level

INTERMEDIATE

Finished Size

11 x 64 inches, including Fringe

Materials

- Kertzer Butterfly Super 10 Multis medium (worsted) weight mercerized 100 per cent cotton yarn (220 yds/100g per ball: 2 skeins #2026 Brazil
- Kertzer Butterfly Super 10 light (DK) weight mercerized 100 per cent cotton yarn (249 yds/125g per skein): 1 skein each #3764 kelly green, #3062 azure, #3724 key lime and #3873 royal
- Light (DK) weight eyelash yarn: 1½ oz/98 yds/50g turquoise
- Bulky (chunky) weight railroad ribbon yarn: 2½ oz/77 yds/50g turquoise/green variegated
- Size K/10½/6.5mm crochet hook or hook needed to obtain gauge

Gauge

3 sts = 1 inch

Pattern Notes

Change colour (see Stitch Guide, p. 31) in last stitch made at end of each row. Fasten off last colour used at end of each row.

Colour sequence is as follows:

Brazil	Key lime	Azure
Kelly green	Turquoise/Green	Royal
Brazil	Turquoise	Brazil
Royal	Turquoise/Green	Kelly green
Azure	Key lime	Brazil

Wrap

Row 1: Working in **back bar** of ch (see illustration), with Brazil (see Pattern Notes for colour sequence), ch 181, sc in 2nd ch from hook, sc in each of next 8 chs, *hdc in next ch, dc in each of next 2 chs, tr in each of next 3 chs, dc in each of next 2 chs, hdc in next ch**, sc in each of next 9 chs, rep from * across, ending last rep at **, **changing colour** (see Pattern Notes) in last st, turn. Fasten off. (180 sts)

Row 2: Ch 1, sc in each st across, turn.

Back Bar of Chain

Row 3: Ch 2 (not counted as st), hdc in first st, *dc in each of next 2 sts, tr in each of next 3 sts, dc in each of next 2 sts, hdc in next st, sc in each of next 9 sts**, hdc in next st, rep from * across, ending last rep at **, turn.

Row 4: Ch 1, sc in each st across, turn.

Row 5: Ch 1, sc in each of first 9 sts, *hdc in next st, dc in each of next 2 sts, tr in each of next 3 sts, dc in each of next 2 sts, hdc in next st**, sc in each of next 9 sts, rep from * across, ending last rep at **, turn.

Next rows: Rep rows 2–5 consecutively, for a total of 31 rows, ending with row 3.

Fringe

Cut 4 strands of each colour except kingfisher, each 14 inches in length. Holding all strands tog as 1, fold in half. Pull fold through end of row, pull ends through fold. Pull to tighten.

Matching colours, place Fringe in end of each row across each short end. Trim ends. ✦

Autumn Wrap

This generous, oversized wrap gives you plenty of style options for a variety of outfits.

DESIGN BY JENNY KING

Skill Level

EASY

Finished Size
One size fits all

Materials
- Light (light worsted) weight yarn: 37 oz/3330 yds/1049g variegated
- Size G/6/4mm crochet hook or size needed to obtain gauge
- Tapestry needle
- Stitch markers

Gauge
3 shells = 3¼ inches; 5 shell rows = 3 inches

Pattern Notes
Weave in loose ends as work progresses.

Join rounds with a slip stitch unless otherwise stated.

Special Stitches
Shell: (2 dc, ch 1, 2 dc) in indicated ch sp.

Beginning shell increase (beg shell inc): (Ch 4, 2 dc, ch 1, 2 dc) in first st.

End shell increase (end shell inc): (2 dc, ch 1, 3 dc) in last st.

Wrap
Row 1: Starting at centre bottom back, ch 5, (2 dc, ch 1, 3 dc) in 5th ch from hook *(4 sk chs count as first dc)*, turn. *(1 shell)*

Row 2 (RS): Ch 4 *(counts as first dc)*, **shell** *(see Special Stitches)* in ch sp of next shell, dc in last st, turn.

Row 3: Beg shell inc *(see Special Stitches)* in first st, shell in ch sp of next shell, **end shell inc** *(see Special Stitches)* in last st, turn. *(3 shells)*

Row 4: Ch 4, shell in ch sp of each shell across to last st, dc in last st, turn.

Row 5: Beg shell inc in first st, shell in ch sp of each shell across to last st, end shell inc in last st, turn. *(5 shells)*

Rows 6–37: [Rep rows 4 and 5 alternately] 16 times.

Row 38: Rep row 4. *(1 dc, 37 shells, 1 dc)*

Rows 39–78: Rep row 4.

First Front
Row 79: Ch 4, shell in ch sp of each of next 15 shells, dc in last st of last worked shell, leaving last 22 shells and dc unworked, turn. *(1 dc, 15 shells, 1 dc)*

Rows 80–148: Rep row 4. At the end of row 148, fasten off. *(1 dc, 15 shells, 1 dc)*

Second Front
Row 79: With RS facing, sk next 7 shells of row 78 for back neck, join with sl st in first dc of 8th shell, ch 4, shell in ch-1 sp of each rem shell across, dc in last st, turn. *(1 dc, 15 shells, 1 dc)*

Rows 80–148: Rep row 4. At the end of row 148, **do not turn**.

Edging
Rnd 1: Working around entire outer edge of Wrap, ch 1, sc in each st and in each ch, 2 sc in end of each dc row around with 3 sc in each corner, join in beg sc.

Rnd 2: Working in **front lps** *(see Stitch Guide, p. 31)*, ch 1, sc in each st around with 3 sc in centre st of each 3-sc corner group, join in beg sc, fasten off. ✦

New Waves Wrap-Ghan

Crocheted in strips, this wrap is large enough to cuddle up in on the coolest evening.

DESIGN BY DARLA SIMS

Skill Level

EASY

Finished Size
Approximately 60 x 74 inches

Materials
- Caron Simply Soft medium (worsted) weight yarn (6 oz/330 yds/170g per skein): 11 skeins #9707 dark sage *(A)*, 4 skeins #9723 raspberry *(D)*
- Caron Simply Soft Brites medium (worsted) weight yarn (6 oz/315 yds/170g per skein): 7 skeins #9607 limelight *(B)*, 6 skeins #9608 blue mint *(C)*
- Size H/8/5mm crochet hook or size needed to obtain gauge
- Tapestry needle
- 10 gold-tone 1-inch buttons
- Sewing needle and matching thread

Gauge
1 wave rep = 3 inches

Pattern Notes
The top edge of this afghan design is buttoned to form sleeves that keep arms warm. Wear it on top for even cozier coverage.

Special Stitch
Shell: 9 tr in st indicated.

Strip A
Make 11.
Row 1 (RS): With C, ch 192 very loosely; sc in 2nd ch from hook; *sk next 4 chs, **shell** (see Special Stitch) in next ch; sk next 4 chs, sc in next ch; rep from * across; ch 4 (counts as a tr); working on opposite side in unused lps of beg ch, 4 tr in unused lp of ch at base of first sc; sc in unused lp of ch at base of next shell: *shell in unused lp of ch at base of next sc; sc in unused lp of ch at base of next shell; rep from * to unused lp of ch at base of last sc; 5 tr in unused lp. (37 shells) Fasten off.
Row 2: Hold piece with RS facing you; join A with sl st in first sc of row 1; ch 4 (counts as a tr), 4 tr in same sc; *sk next 3 tr, sc in next 3 tr, sk next 3 tr, working over next sc, shell in same sp as sc made; rep from * 17 times; sk next 3 tr, sc in next 3 tr, sk next 3 tr, 5 tr in next sc. Fasten off.
Row 3: Hold piece with RS facing you and unworked edge of row 1 at top; with A, make slip knot on hook and join with sc in 4th ch of beg ch-4 at right-hand edge; sc in next tr, sk next 3 tr; *working over next sc, shell in same sp as

sc made; sk next 3 tr, sc in next 3 tr, sk next 3 tr; rep from * to last sc; shell in last sc; sk next 3 tr, sc in last 2 tr. Fasten off.
Row 4: Hold piece with RS facing you and row 2 at top; with B, make slip knot on hook and join with sc in 4th ch of beg ch-4 of row 2; sc in each rem st. Fasten off.
Row 5: Hold piece with RS facing you and row 3 at top; with B, make slip knot on hook and join with sc in first sc of row 3; sc in each rem st.
Fasten off and weave in all ends.

Strip B
Make 10.
Row 1 (RS): With D, rep row 1 of Strip A.
Rows 2–5: Rep rows 2–5 of Strip A.

Assembly
Beg with Strip A, with tapestry needle and A, sew Strips tog through **back lps** (see Stitch Guide, p. 31) only, alternating Strips.

Side Edging
Hold piece with RS facing you and 1 long side at top; with B, make slip knot on hook and join with sc in edge of first row at right-hand edge; working across side, work 224 sc evenly spaced to last row. Fasten off.

Rep on opposite long side.

Border
Rnd 1 (RS): Hold afghan with RS facing you and 1 short end at top; with B, make slip knot on hook and join with sc in first sc in upper right-hand corner; 2 sc in same sc—beg corner made; working across side, sc in each sc to last sc; 3 sc in last sc—corner made; working across next side, sc in each sc; working across next side, 3 sc in first sc—corner made; sc in each sc to last sc of side; 3 sc in last sc—corner made; working across next side, sc in each sc to first sc; join with sl st in first sc.
Rnd 2: Ch 1, sc in same sc; 3 sc in next sc—corner made; *sc in each sc to 2nd sc of next corner; 3 sc in 2nd sc—corner made; rep from * twice; sc in each sc to first sc; join with sl st in first sc.
Fasten off and weave in ends.

Finishing
Fold over 3 Strips (or number of strips required for comfortable fit) from top of afghan. Sew buttons evenly spaced on WS of corresponding Strip to form armholes/sleeves, placing first button approximately 13–15 inches from top edge. Use spaces between tr of shells for buttonholes. ◆

Tasteful Tweed

Ruanas are the new ponchos, and this one's got style! A purple tweed yarn makes it versatile to wear with anything.

DESIGN BY DEB RICHEY FOR CARON INTERNATIONAL

Skill Level

◐■☐☐
EASY

Finished Size
26 inches across back x 30 inches long

Materials
- Caron Simply Soft Tweed medium (worsted) weight yarn (3 oz/159 yds/85g per skein): 7 skeins #0008 grape
- Sizes I/9/5.5mm and J/10/6mm crochet hooks or size needed to obtain gauge

Gauge
Size I hook: 1 shell and 1 dc in pattern = 2¼ inches

Special Stitches
Shell: (Sc, {ch 6, sc} 3 times) in next st or ch.
Picot chain (picot ch): Ch 3, sc in 2nd ch from hook, ch 2.

Back
Row 1: With size I hook, ch 103, dc in 3rd ch from hook, [ch 4, sk next 4 chs, **shell** *(see Special Stitches)* in next ch, ch 4, sk next

4 chs, dc in next ch] across, turn. *(11 dc, 10 shells)*

Row 2: Ch 1, sc in first st, *ch 1, [sc in next ch-6 of shell, ch 3] twice, sc in next ch-6 of same shell, ch 1, sc in next dc, rep from * across, turn. *(41 sc, 20 ch-3 sps, 20 ch-1 sps)*

Row 3: Ch 1, (sc, {ch 6, sc} twice) in first st, [ch 4, sk next sc, dc in next sc, ch 4, sk next sc, shell in next sc] 9 times, ch 4, sk next sc, dc in next sc, ch 4, sk next sc, (sc, ch 6, sc, ch 4, sc) in last st, turn. *(9 shells)*

Row 4: Ch 1, sc in first ch-4 sp, ch 3, sc in next ch-6 sp, *ch 1, sc in next dc, ch 1, [sc in next ch-6 sp, ch 3] twice, sc in next ch-6 sp, rep from * 8 times, ch 1, sc in next dc, ch 1, sc in next ch-6 sp, ch 3, sc in last ch-6 sp, turn. *(41 sc, 20 ch-3 sps, 20 ch-1 sps)*

Row 5: Ch 2 *(does not count as st)*, dc in first st, [ch 4, sk next sc, shell in next sc, ch 4, sk next sc, dc in next sc] across, turn. *(11 dc, 10 shells)*

Rows 6–58: [Rep rows 2-5 consecutively] 13 times ending with row 2.

First Front

Row 1: With size I hook, ch 1, (sc, {ch 6, sc} twice) in first st, [ch 4, sk next sc, dc in next sc, ch 4, sk next sc, shell in next sc] 3 times, ch 4, sk next sc, dc in next sc, ch 4, sk next sc, (sc, ch 6, sc, ch 4, sc) in next st, leaving rem sts

unworked, turn. *(3 shells)*

Row 2: Ch 1, sc in first ch-4 sp, ch 3, sc in next ch-6 sp, *ch 1, sc in next dc, ch 1, [sc in next ch-6 sp, ch 3] twice, sc in next ch-6 sp, rep from * 3 times, ch 1, sc in next dc, ch 1, sc in next ch-6 sp, ch 3, sc in last ch-6 sp, turn. *(17 sc, 8 ch-3 sps)*

Row 3 Ch 2, dc in first st, [ch 4, sk next sc, shell in next sc, ch 4, sk next sc, dc in next sc] across, turn. *(4 shells)*

Row 4: Ch 1, sc in first st, *ch 1, [sc in next ch-6 of shell, ch 3] twice, sc in next ch-6 of same shell, ch 1, sc in next dc, rep from * across, turn. *(17 sc, 8 ch-3 sps)*

Row 5: Ch 1, (sc, {ch 6, sc} twice) in first st, [ch 4, sk next sc, dc in next sc, ch 4, sk next sc, shell in next sc] 3 times, ch 4, sk next sc, dc in next sc, ch 4, sk next sc, (sc, ch 6, sc, ch 4, sc) in last st, turn. *(3 shells)*

Rows 6–57: [Rep rows 2-5 consecutively] 13 times. Fasten off at end of last row.

Second Front

Row 1: Sk sts above next 2 shells on row 58 of Back, with size I hook, join with sc in st above next dc, (ch 6, sc) twice in same st, [ch 4, sk next sc, dc in next sc, ch 4, sk next sc, shell in next sc] 3 times, ch 4, sk next sc, dc in next sc, ch 4, sk next sc, (sc, ch 6, sc, ch 4, sc) in next st. *(3 shells)*

Rows 2–57: Rep rows 2–57 of First Front.

Edging

Rnd 1: With size J hook, working around entire outer edge, join with sc in any st, **picot ch** *(see Special Stitches, p. 83)*, evenly sp (sc, picot ch) around, join with sl st in beg sc.

Rnd 2: Sl st in next ch, sl st in next picot, picot ch, (sc, picot ch) in each picot around with (ch 2, dc, ch 2) at each inside corner, join with sl st in beg sc.

Rnd 3: Sl st in next ch, sl st in next picot, ch 1, (dc, sc, picot ch) in same picot and in each picot around with (ch 2, dc, ch 2) in each inside corner, join with sl st in beg dc. Fasten off. ✦

Flower Power

This fun cotton shawl is perfect to ward off the chill of cool summer evenings.

DESIGN BY MARY BETH TEMPLE

Skill Level

EASY

Finished Sizes
Shawl: 30 inches deep x 75 inches wide
Pin: 6 inches across

Materials
- Tahki Cotton Classic light (light worsted) weight yarn (1¾ oz/108 yds/50g per skein): 9 skeins #3764 bright spearmint, 2 skeins #3001 white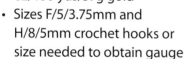
- Medium (worsted) weight cotton yarn: 2 oz/100 yds/57g gold
- Sizes F/5/3.75mm and H/8/5mm crochet hooks or size needed to obtain gauge
- Tapestry needle
- Sewing needle
- Pin back
- White sewing thread
- Stitch markers

Gauge
Size H hook: 4 shells = 4 inches; 7 pattern rows = 3½ inches

Pattern Note
Join with a slip stitch unless otherwise stated.

Flower

Centre
Make 14.
Rnd 1: With size F hook and gold, ch 3, join in beg ch to form ring, ch 1, 5 sc in ring, join in beg sc. *(5 sc)*
Rnd 2: Ch 1, 2 sc in first st, 2 sc in each st around, join in beg sc. *(10 sc)*
Rnd 3: Ch 1, sc in first st, 2 sc in next st, [sc in next st, 2 sc in next st] around, join in beg sc. *(15 sc)*
Rnd 4: Ch 1, sc in first st, 2 sc in each of next 2 sts, [sc in next st, 2 sc in each of next 2 sts] around, join in beg sc. Fasten off. *(25 sc)*

Petals
Row 1: With size F hook and white, join with sc in any st, sc in each of next 4 sts, turn. *(5 sc)*
Row 2: Ch 2 *(counts as first hdc)*, hdc in each of next 4 sts, turn. *(5 hdc)*
Row 3: Ch 3 *(counts as first dc)*, dc in each st across, turn. *(5 dc)*
Row 4: Ch 2, hdc in each of next 4 sts, turn. *(5 hdc)*
Row 5: Ch 1, sc in each st across, turn. *(5 sc)*
Row 6: Ch 1, **sc dec** *(see Stitch Guide, p. 31)* in first 2 sts, sc in next st, sc dec in last 2 sts, turn. *(3 sc)*

Row 7: Ch 1, sc dec in next 3 sts. Fasten off.
Working in next 5 sts on last row of Centre, rep Petal 4 times.

Shawl

Row 1: With size H hook and kelly, join with sc in tip of any Petal on 1 Flower, ch 12, sc in tip of any Petal on another Flower, turn. *(12 chs, 2 sc)*
Row 2: (Ch 3, 2 dc) in first sc, [ch 1, 3 dc in ch-12 sp] 3 times, ch 1, 3 dc in last sc, turn. *(5 3-dc groups)*
Rows 3–8: (Ch 3, 2 dc) in first st, working in sps between 3-dc groups, [ch 1, 3 dc in next sp] across, ch 1, 3 dc in last st. *(11 3-dc groups)*
Row 9: Ch 3, sl st in tip of any Petal on another Flower, 2 dc in same st on last row, working in sps between 3-dc groups, [ch 1, 3 dc in next sp] across, ch 1, 3 dc in last st, sl st in tip of any Petal on another Flower, turn. *(12 3-dc groups)*
Rows 10–17: (Ch 3, 2 dc) in first st, working in sps between 3-dc groups, [ch 1, 3 dc in next sp] across, ch 1, 3 dc in last st. *(20 3-dc groups at end of last row)*
Row 18: Ch 3, sl st in tip of any Petal on another Flower, 2 dc in

same st on last row, working in sps between 3-dc groups, [ch 1, 3 dc in next sp] across, ch 1, 3 dc in last st, sl st in tip of any Petal on another Flower, turn. *(21 3-dc groups)*

Rows 19–54: [Rep rows 10-18 consecutively] 4 times. *(57 3-dc groups at end of last row)*

Row 55: Ch 2, hdc in each st across. Fasten off.

Tack tog first free Petals below each joining tog on each side of Shawl.

Polka Dot

Make 6 each gold and white.

Rnd 1: With size F hook, ch 3, join in beg ch to form ring, ch 1, 5 sc in ring, join in beg sc. *(5 sc)*

Rnd 2: Ch 1, 2 sc in first sts, 2 sc in each st around, join in beg sc. *(10 sc)*

Rnd 3: Ch 1, sc in first st, 2 sc in next st, [sc in next st, 2 sc in next st] around, join in beg sc. *(15 sc)*

Rnd 4: Ch 1, sc in first st, 2 sc in each of next 2 sts, [sc in next st, 2 sc in each of next 2 sts] around, join in beg sc. *(25 sc)*

Rnd 5: Ch 1, sc in first st, [2 sc in next st, sc in each of next 2 sts] around, join in beg sc. Fasten off. Alternating colours of Polka Dots, sew 1 side of 1 Dot to Petals where tacked tog and other side

of Dot to corresponding row on Shawl. Continue until all joinings of Petals have 1 Polka Dot *(see photo)*.

Pin

Centre

Rnd 1: With size F hook and gold, ch 3, join in beg ch to form ring, ch 1, 5 sc in ring, join in beg sc. *(5 sc)*

Rnd 2: Ch 1, 2 sc in first st, 2 sc in each st around, join in beg sc. *(10 sc)*

Rnd 3: Ch 1, sc in first st, 2 sc in next st, [sc in next st, 2 sc in next st] around, join in beg sc. *(15 sc)*

Rnd 4: Ch 1, sc in first st, 2 sc in each of next 2 sts, [sc in next st, 2 sc in each of next 2 sts] around, join in beg sc. Fasten off. *(25 sc)*

Petals

Row 1: With size F hook and white, join with sc in any st, sc in each of next 4 sts, turn. *(5 sc)*

Row 2: Ch 2 *(counts as first hdc),* hdc in each of next 4 sts, turn. *(5 hdc)*

Row 3: Ch 3 *(counts as first dc),* dc in each st across, turn. *(5 dc)*

Row 4: Ch 2, hdc in each of next 4 sts, turn. *(5 hdc)*

Row 5: Ch 1, sc in each st across, turn. *(5 sc)*

Row 6: Ch 1, **sc dec** *(see Stitch Guide, p. 31)* in first 2 sts, sc in next st, sc dec in last 2 sts, turn. *(3 sc)*

Row 7: Ch 1, sc dec in next 3 sts. Fasten off.

Working in next 5 sts on last row of Centre, rep Petal 4 times.

With sewing needle and thread, sew pin back to back of Flower. ✦

Peach Sensation Poncho

Create a carefree, casual look in this chic, diagonal-design poncho that features single-shoulder straps adorned with a large, trendy flower.

DESIGN BY RAYNELDA CALDERON

Skill Level

INTERMEDIATE

Finished Size
One size fits most

Materials
- Caron Simply Soft medium (worsted) weight yarn (6 oz/330 yds/170g per skein): 3 skeins #9737 light country peach
- Caron Simply Soft medium (worsted) weight yarn (3 oz/165 yds/85g per skein): 1 skein #2601 white
- Size H/8/5mm crochet hook or size needed to obtain gauge
- Tapestry needle

Gauge
7 sts = 2 inches, 4 rows in pattern = 1½ inches
Check gauge to save time.

Poncho

Row 1: With light country peach, ch 63, dc in 3rd ch from hook *(first 2 chs do not count as st)*, ch 1, dc in same ch, *[sk next ch, sc in next ch, sk next ch, (dc, ch 1, dc) in next ch] twice, ch 10, sk next 6 chs, (dc, ch 1, dc) in next ch, rep from * across, turn.

(4 ch-10 sps, 8 sc, 13 ch-1 sps)

Row 2: Ch 2 *(does not count as st)*, sc in first ch-1 sp, ch 10, *sc in next ch-1 sp, (dc, ch 1, dc) in next sc, sc in next ch-1 sp, (dc, ch 1, dc) in next sc, sc in next ch-1 sp**, ch 10, rep from * across, ending last rep at **, turn. *(4 ch-10 sps, 8 ch-1 sps, 13 sc)*

Row 3: Ch 4 *(counts as first dc and ch-1 sp)*, dc in same st, *sc in next ch-1 sp, (dc, ch 1, dc) in next sc, sc in next ch-1 sp, (dc, ch 1, dc) in next sc, ch 10, (dc, ch 1, dc) in next sc, rep from * across, turn.

Row 4: Ch 2, sc in first ch-1 sp, *ch 5, sc around all 3 ch-10 chs of previous 3 rows, ch 5, [sc in next ch-1 sp, (dc, ch 1, dc) in next sc] twice, sc in next ch-1 sp, rep from * across, turn.

Row 5: Ch 4, dc in same st, *[sc in next ch-1 sp, (dc, ch 1, dc) in next sc] twice, ch 10, sk next sc, (dc, ch 1, dc) in next sc, rep from * across, turn.

Row 6: Ch 2, sc in first ch-1 sp, ch 10, *[sc in next ch-1 sp, (dc, ch 1, dc) in next sc] twice, sc in next ch-1 sp**, ch 10, rep from * across, ending last rep at **, turn.

Row 7: Ch 4, dc in same st, *[sc in next ch-1 sp, (dc, ch 1, dc) in next sc] twice, ch 10, (dc,

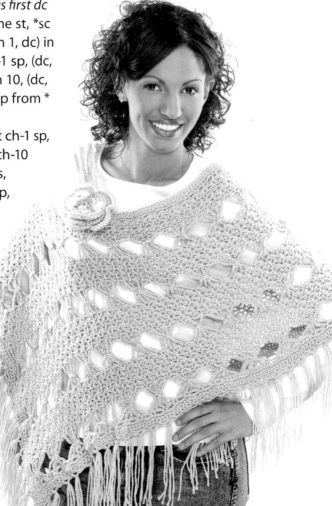

ch 1, dc) in next sc, rep from * across, turn.

Row 8: Ch 2, sc in first ch-1 sp, ch 10, *[sc in next ch-1 sp, (dc, ch 1, dc) in next sc] twice, sc in next ch-1 sp**, ch 10, rep from * across, ending last rep at **, turn.

Row 9: Ch 4, dc in same st, *[sc in next ch-1 sp, (dc, ch 1, dc) in next sc] twice, ch 5, sc around all 4 ch-10 chs of previous 4 rows, ch 5, (dc, ch 1, dc) in next sc, rep from * across, turn.

Rows 10–13: [Rep rows 2 and 3 alternately] twice.

Row 14: Ch 2, sc in first ch-1 sp, *ch 5, sc around all 4 ch-10 chs of previous 4 rows, ch 5, [sc in next ch-1 sp, (dc, ch 1, dc) in next sc] twice, sc in next ch-1 sp, rep from * across, turn.

Rows 15–114: [Rep rows 5-14 consecutively] 10 times

Border

Rnd 115: Now working in rnds, ch 2, evenly sp 70 sc across each short edge and 200 sc in ends of rows down each long edge with (sc, ch 1, sc) in each corner, join with sl st in beg sc, **turn.**

Rnds 116 & 117: Ch 1, sc in each st around with (sc, ch 1, sc) in each corner ch sp, join, **turn.** At end of last rnd, fasten off. Fold in half and sew about 8 inches tog from edge for underarm.

Trim

Working around outer edge, join light country peach with sc in

seam, ch 1, sk next st or ch, [sc in next st or ch, ch 1, sk next st or ch] around, join with sl st in beg sc. Fasten off.

Fringe

Cut 2 strands of light country peach yarn 12 inches in length. Holding strands tog, fold strands in half, pull fold through ch sp, pull ends through fold. Pull to tighten.
Fringe in every other ch-1 sp around outer edge. Trim ends.

Shoulder Strap
Make 4.

Holding 1 strand of light country peach and white tog as 1, ch 65. Fasten off.
Sew shoulder strap ends to each side of Poncho side by side with the first strap 5 inches from underarm seam.

Flower

Rnd 1 (RS): With white, ch 5, sl st in first ch to form ring, ch 1, 8 sc in ring, join with sl st in beg sc. *(8 sc)*

Rnd 2: [Ch 5, sl st in next st] around, join with sl st in base of beg ch-5, **turn.** *(8 ch-5 sps)*

Rnd 3 (WS): Working behind ch-5 sps and same sts of rnd 1, ch 6, sl st in next sc of rnd 1, [ch 6, sk next sc on rnd 1, sl st in next sc on rnd 1] around, ch 6, join with sl st in base of beg ch-6. *(5 ch-6 sps)*

Rnd 4: Working in ch-6 sps, ch 2, 5 dc in first ch sp, ch 2, sl st in same ch sp, (5 dc, ch 2, sl st) in each ch sp around, join with sl st in base of beg ch-2. Fasten off.

Rnd 5: Working in front of petals on last rnd, join light country peach with sl st in any sl st, ch 7, [sl st in next sl st, ch 7] around, join with sl st in beg sl st.

Rnd 6: (Sl st, ch 2, 8 dc) in each ch-7 sp around, join with sl st in beg sl st, **turn.**

Rnd 7 (RS): Working behind petals of last rnd, ch 9, [sl st in next sl st, ch 9] around, join.

Rnd 8: (Sl st, ch 2, 10 dc) in each ch-9 sp around, join. Fasten off.

Rnd 9: Working in chs of ch-5 sps on rnd 2, join light country peach with sl st in any ch, sl st in each ch around, join. Fasten off.

Rnd 10: Working in top of petals on rnd 4, join with sl st in any st, sl st in each st and ch around, join. Fasten off.

Rnd 11: Working in top of petals on rnd 10, join white with sl st in any st, sl st in each st and ch around, join. Fasten off.
Sew Flower to front at base of Shoulder Straps as shown in photo. ◆

Hooded Riding Shawlcho

Is it a shawl? A poncho? It's both! Light like a shawl, hooded like a poncho—this is a marvellous and unique design!

DESIGN BY LANA BENNETT

Skill Level

INTERMEDIATE

Finished Size
One size fits most
63 inches wide x 28 inches long, excluding hood

Materials
- Bernat Soft Bouclé bulky (chunky) weight yarn (5 oz/225 yds/140g per ball): 3 balls #26948 slate shades
- Size M/13/9mm crochet hook or size needed to obtain gauge
- Yarn needle
- Sewing needle
- Sewing thread
- 3 (1-inch) buttons

Gauge
3 dc = 1 inch; 1 dc = 1 inch
Check gauge to save time.

Pattern Notes
Weave in loose ends as work progresses.

Join rounds with a slip stitch unless otherwise stated.

Special Stitch
Half double crochet decrease (hdc dec): [Yo hook, insert hook in next st, yo, draw up a lp] twice, yo, draw through all 5 lps on hook.

Shawl
Row 1: Beg at bottom edge, ch 54, dc in 3rd ch from hook, dc in each rem ch across, turn. *(52 dc)*
Row 2: Ch 2 *(counts as first dc throughout)*, dc in same st as beg ch-2, dc in each st across to last st, 2 dc in last st, turn. *(54 dc)*
Rows 3–33: Rep row 2. *(116 dc)*

Edging
Rnd 34: Now working in rnds, ch 1, work 60 hdc evenly spaced down side edge of Shawl, working across opposite side of foundation ch, **hdc dec** *(see Special Stitch)* over next 2 sts, hdc in each of next 48 sts, hdc dec over next 2 sts, work 60 hdc up side edge of shawl, ch 1, hdc in each hdc across row 33, join in beg hdc.
Row 35: Now working in rows, ch 2, [hdc in next hdc, ch 1] down side edge, across bottom edge and up opposite side edge.

Hood
Row 36: Working across top edge, sl st in each of next 34 sts, ch 2, working in **front lps** *(see Stitch Guide, p. 31)* only, dc in each of next 47 sts, turn. *(48 dc)*
Row 37: Ch 2, dc in each of next 47 dc, turn. *(48 dc)*
Rows 38–50: Rep row 37.
Row 51: Rep row 37, leaving a 15-inch length, fasten off.

Fold row 51 in half. With rem length, matching sts, sew across edge, secure and fasten off.

Front Trim
Row 1: Attach yarn to right front bottom edge in corner ch-1 sp, ch 2, hdc in next ch-1 sp, [ch 1, hdc in next ch-1 sp] up right front to row 36 of Hood, working in side edge of rows, [ch 1, hdc in side edge of next row] around Hood edge, working down left front, [ch 1, hdc in next ch-1 sp] down right front to corner, fasten off.

Finishing
Using natural sps between sts for buttonholes on right front, attach first button at left front in line with row 36 of Hood, sk next 10 hdc from first button and attach next button, sk next 10 hdc from 2nd button and attach 3rd button. ◆

From-Elegant-to-Casual Cozy Capelet

This fun, flirty little capelet can easily go from daytime chic to evening elegance.

DESIGN BY NAZANIN FARD

Skill Level

INTERMEDIATE

Finished Size

Approximately 15 inches long

Materials

- Patons Bohemian super bulky (super chunky) weight yarn (2¾ oz/ 68 yds/80g per ball): 5 balls #11110 indigo indulgence **6 SUPER BULKY**
- Size N/13/9mm crochet hook or size needed to obtain gauge
- Tapestry needle
- ¾-inch button in matching colour
- Sewing needle and matching thread

Gauge

12 dc = 4 inches

Capelet

Row 1: Ch 51, dc in 3rd ch from hook *(beg 2 sk chs count as dc)* and in each ch across, turn. *(50 dc)*

Row 2: Ch 2 *(counts as dc throughout)*, *2 dc in next dc, dc in next dc; rep from * to beg 2 sk chs, 2 dc in 2nd ch of beg 2 sk chs, turn. *(75 dc)*

Row 3: Ch 2, dc in each dc across, turn.

Row 4: Ch 2, *2 dc in next dc, dc in next dc; rep from * across, turn. *(112 dc)*

Rows 5–15: Rep row 3. Fasten off and weave in all ends.

Finishing

Sew button on 1 side of the front on row 1. Use dc across from the button as a buttonhole. ✦

Colourful Winter Wrap

When there's a chill in the air, drape this snugly and light-as-a-feather, but warm-as-toast wrap over your shoulders.

DESIGN BY KATHERINE ENG

Skill Level

BEGINNER

Finished Size

14 x 58 inches, excluding Fringe

Materials

- Plymouth Yarns Encore Boucle bulky (chunky) weight yarn (3½ oz/101 yds/100g per ball): 3 balls #7132 turquoise/gold/magenta variegated
- Plymouth Yarns Encore Chunky bulky (chunky) weight yarn (3½ oz/143 yds/100g per ball): 1 ball #7132 turquoise/gold/magenta variegated
- Size P/15mm crochet hook or size needed to obtain gauge
- Tapestry needle

Gauge

Sc, [ch 2, sc] twice = 4 inches; rows 1–3 = 2½ inches

Pattern Notes

Weave in loose ends as work progresses.

Leave a 7-inch length at beginning and when fastening off to tie into Fringe.

First Half

Row 1 (WS): With A, ch 104, sc in 2nd ch from hook, [ch 2, sk next 2 chs, sc in next ch] across, turn. *(35 sc, 34 ch-2 sps)*

Row 2 (RS): Ch 1, (sc, ch 2, sc) in first sc, [ch 1, sk next ch-2 sp, (sc, ch 2, sc) in next sc] across, turn. *(35 ch-2 sps)*

Row 3: Sl st into ch-2 sp, ch 1, sc in same ch-2 sp, [ch 2, sc in next ch-2 sp] across, turn. *(35 sc, 34 ch-2 sps)*

Row 4: Rep row 2, fasten off.

Row 5: Draw up a lp of B in first ch-2 sp, ch 1, sc in same ch-2 sp, [ch 2, sc in next ch-2 sp] across, turn.

Row 6: Rep row 2.

Row 7: Rep row 3.

Row 8: Rep row 2.

Row 9: Draw up a lp of A in first ch-2 sp, ch 1, sc in same ch-2 sp, [ch 2, sc in next ch-2 sp] across, turn.

Row 10: Rep row 2.

Row 11: Rep row 3.

Row 12: Rep row 2.

Second Half

Row 1 (WS): Working on opposite side of foundation ch of First Half, draw up a lp of A in first ch, ch 1, sc in same ch, [ch 2, sk next 2 chs, sc in next ch] across, turn. *(35 sc, 34 ch-2 sps)*

Rows 2–12: Rep rows 2–12 of First Half.

Fringe

Cut 14-inch lengths of A and B to match ends of rows. Add 1 length to tails and 2 lengths where there are none.

Fold lengths in half and tie with tails in an overhand knot. Trim ends to 5 inches. ✦

Bonny Blue Hooded Blanket

A richly textured fabric, created with an interesting picot shell stitch, adds cozy warmth to this adorable hooded blanket that ties together to form a bunting-like wrap.

DESIGN BY CORA RATTLE

Skill Level
■■□□
EASY

Size
26 x 26 inches, excluding Hood

Materials
• Bernat Baby Coordinates fine (baby) weight yarn (6 oz/431 yds/ 160g per skein): 6 skeins #01009 soft blue
• Size H/8/5mm crochet hook or size needed to obtain gauge
• Yarn needle
• 36 inches (½-inch-wide) baby blue ribbon
• Sewing needle
• Thread

Gauge
Picot shell = 1 inch; 2 rows = 1 inch
Check gauge to save time.

Pattern Notes
Weave in loose ends as work progresses.

Work with two strands of yarn held together throughout.

Special Stitch
Picot shell: (Sc, ch 3, 2 dc, ch 3, sl st in top of last dc, dc) in same st.

Blanket
Row 1: Beg at top edge of blanket, ch 99, **picot shell** *(see Special Stitch)* in 2nd ch from hook, [sk next 3 chs, picot shell in next ch] 23 times, sc in last ch, turn. *(24 picot shells)*
Row 2: Ch 3 *(counts as first dc throughout)*, [work **dc dec** *(see Stitch Guide, p. 31)*, ch 3, sc over next ch-3 sp] across, turn.
Row 3: Ch 1, picot shell in first sc, [picot shell in next sc] across, ending with sc in 3rd ch of ch-3.
Rows 4–52: [Rep rows 2 and 3 alternately] 25 times, ending last rep at row 2. At end of last rep, fasten off.

Hood
Row 1: With top edge of blanket facing *(opposite side of foundation ch)*, mark off centre 12 picot shells of row 1, leaving first and last 6 shells free, attach yarn, ch 1, picot shell in same st, [sk 3 chs, picot shell in next ch] 11 times, sk 3 chs, sc in next ch, turn. *(12 picot shells)*
Rows 2–12: [Rep rows 2 and 3 of blanket alternately] 6 times, ending last rep at row 2. At the end of row 12, fasten off.
Thread one strand of yarn onto yarn needle. With WS facing, fold hood in half; sew across edge. Turn hood right side out.

Finishing
Place hooded blanket on a flat surface with hood at centre top, fold both outer edges to centre. Cut ribbon in half. Pass end of ribbon through side edge of 6th row at centre from top edge of blanket, turn raw edge under and sew to edge of ribbon. Sew second length of ribbon on opposite edge at centre front. Tie ribbon ends in a bow. ◆

Hearts for Baby

Rows of pastel hearts surrounded by lacy white shells create the simple join-as-you-go strips in this sweetheart of a blanket.

DESIGN BY KAY LEMASTER

Skill Level
■■□□
EASY

Finished Size
46 x 50 inches

Materials
- Red Heart Baby Econo medium (worsted) weight yarn (pompadour 6 oz/480 yds/170g per skein): 3 skeins #1001 white, 1 skein each #1570 lavender, #1722 light pink, #1802 baby blue, #1224 baby yellow, #1680 pastel green and #1047 candy print
- Size G/6/4mm crochet hook or size needed to obtain gauge

Gauge
Heart = 2 inches wide

Pattern Notes
Beginning chain-3 counts as first double crochet.

Join with a slip stitch unless otherwise stated.

First Strip
Row 1: For **first heart**, with lavender, ch 8, 3 tr in fourth ch from hook, tr in next ch, dc in next ch, hdc in next ch, 3 sc in last ch; working on opposite side of ch, hdc in next ch, dc in next ch, tr in next ch, (3 tr, ch 3, sl st) in last ch, **do not join**. *(15 sts, 2 ch-3 sps)*

Rows 2–30: For **next hearts**, ch 8, 3 tr in fourth ch from hook, tr in next ch, dc in next ch, hdc in next ch, sc in last ch; working on opposite side of ch, 2 sc in same ch as last sc, hdc in next ch, dc in next ch, tr in next ch, (3 tr, ch 3, sl st) in last ch, do not join. Fasten off at end of last row.

Edging
Rnd 1: Join white with sc in centre st of 3-sc group at bottom of first heart, 3 sc in same st, ch 3, sk next 3 sts, sc in each of next 3 sts, [ch 3, sc in each of first 3 tr on next heart side] across, ch 2, sc in first ch of next ch-3, ch 2, 3 sc in centre of heart, ch 2, sc in third ch of next ch 3, ch 2, sc in last 3 tr of same heart side, [ch 3, sc in each of last 3 tr in next heart side] across, ch 3, join in beg sc. *(189 sc, 60 ch-3 sps, 4 ch-2 sps)*

Rnd 2: Ch 1, 2 sc in first st, sc in each st and in each ch around, join in beg sc. Fasten off. *(378 sc)*

Rnd 3: Join candy print with sc in centre top st on Strip, ch 3, dc in side of last sc made, sk next 2 sts, [sc in next st, ch 3, dc in side of last sc made, sk next 2 sts] around, join in beg sc. Fasten off. *(126 ch sps, 126 sc)*

Rnd 4: Join white in first sc, ch 3, 6 dc in same st, sc in next sc, [7 dc in next sc, sc in next sc] around, join in third ch of beg ch-3.

Second Strip
With light pink, work same as First Strip.

Edging
Rnds 1–3: Work same as rnds 1-3 of First Strip Edging.

Rnd 4: Join white in first sc, ch 3, 6 dc in same st, sc in next sc, 7 sc in next sc, [sc in next sc, 2 dc in next sc, insert hook in same sc, yo, pull lp through, yo, pull through 2 lps on hook, insert hook in centre st of corresponding 7-dc group on last Strip, yo, pull through st and lps on hook, 4 dc in same st on this Strip] 29 times, sc in next sc, [7 dc in next sc, sc in next sc] around, join in third ch of beg ch-3. Fasten off. Working in colour sequence of baby blue, baby yellow, pastel green, lavender and light pink, work Second Strip and Edging eight more times, ending with pastel green Strip and a total of ten Strips. ◆

It's a Girl!

With ribbons and ruffles in pretty pink and white, this afghan is perfect for someone small and sweet.

DESIGN BY PEGGY BOCK

Skill Level
⬛⬛⬜⬜⬜
EASY

Finished Size
32 x 36½ inches

Materials
- Red Heart Super Saver medium (worsted) weight yarn (7 oz/364 yds/198g per skein): 3 skeins #311 white, 1 skein #724 baby pink
- Size J/10/6mm crochet hook or size needed to obtain gauge

Gauge
12 dc = 4 inches; 3 dc rows and 8 sc rows = 4 inches

Blanket
Row 1: With white, ch 85, dc in 4th ch from hook and in each ch across, turn. Fasten off. *(83 dc)*
Row 2: Join baby pink with sc in first st, sc in each st across, turn. *(83 sc)*
Row 3: Ch 1, sc in each st across, turn. Fasten off.
Row 4: Join white with sc in first st, sc in each of next 2 sts, [**fpdc** *(see Stitch Guide, p. 31)* around corresponding st 3 rows below, sk next st on last row behind post st, sc in each of next 3 sts] across, turn. *(83 sts)*
Row 5: Ch 3 *(counts as first dc)*, dc in each st across, turn. Fasten off.
Rows 6 & 7: Rep rows 2 and 3.
Row 8: Join white with sc in first st, [fpdc around corresponding st 3 rows below, sk next st on last row behind post st, sc in each of next 3 sts] across to last 2 sts, fpdc around corresponding st 3 rows below, sk next st on last row behind post st, sc in last st, turn. *(83 sts)*
Row 9: Ch 3, dc in each st across, turn. Fasten off. *(83 dc)*
Rows 10–93: [Rep rows 2-9 consecutively] 11 times, ending last rep at row 5. **Do not fasten off** at end of last row.

Border
Rnd 1: Ch 1, 3 sc in first st, sc in each st across with 3 sc in last st, evenly sp 95 sc across ends of rows, working in starting ch on opposite side of row 1, 3 sc in first ch, sc in each ch across with 3 sc in last ch, evenly sp 95 sc across ends of rows, join with sl st in beg sc. Fasten off. *(83 sc on each short end between centre corner sts, 97 sc on each long edge between centre corner sts)*
Rnd 2: Join baby pink with sc in first centre corner st, (ch 2, sc) in same st, *ch 1, sk next st, [sc in next st, ch 1, sk next st] across to next centre corner st**, (sc, ch 2, sc) in next corner st, rep from * around, ending last rep at **, join with sl st in beg sc. Fasten off.
Rnd 3: Join white with sc in any corner ch sp, 2 sc in same sp, ch 1, (sc, ch 1) in each ch sp around with (3 sc, ch 1) in each corner ch sp, join with sl st in beg sc.
Rnd 4: Ch 4 *(counts as first tr)*, tr in same st, 2 tr in each st around with 3 tr in each ch sp, join with sl st in 4th ch of beg ch-4.
Rnd 5: Sl st in each st around, join with sl st in joining sl st of last rnd. Fasten off.

Bows
With baby pink, ch 20, sl st around 1 centre corner st on rnd 2, ch 20. Fasten off. Tie ends into a Bow.

Rep on each corner of rnd 2. ✦

Swirly-Fringed Blanket

Cute little corkscrew curls add a fun, fanciful touch to this sweet and simple little blanket.

DESIGN BY KAREN HAY

Skill Level

EASY

Finished Size

Approximately 48 x 48 inches, including spiral edging

Materials

- Bernat Baby Coordinates Sweet Stripes light (light worsted) weight yarn (5¼ oz/404 yds/150g per skein): 3 skeins #09414 candy stripes
- Size H/8/5mm crochet hook or size needed to obtain gauge
- Tapestry needle

Gauge

In pattern: 14 sts = 4 inches

Blanket

Row 1: Ch 149; sc in 2nd ch from hook, dc in next ch; *sc in next ch, dc in next ch, rep from * across, turn. *(148 sts)*

Row 2: Ch 17, 2 dc in 3rd ch from hook and in each of next 14 chs— *spiral made;* *sc in next dc, dc in next sc; rep from * across, turn.

Row 3: Rep row 2.

Row 4: Ch 1, sc in first dc, dc in next sc; * sc in next dc, dc in next sc; rep from * across, turn.

Rows 5 & 6: Rep row 4.

Rep rows 2–6 until piece measures approximately 42 inches from beg.

Last row: Ch 1, sc in first dc, dc in next sc; *ch 17, 2 dc in 3rd ch from hook and in each of next 14 chs—*spiral made;* [sc in next dc, dc in next sc] twice; rep from * to last 2 sts; ch 17, 2 dc in 3rd ch from hook and in each of next 14 chs—*spiral made;* sc in next dc, dc in last sc.

Fasten off and weave in ends.

Lower Edging

Hold piece with RS facing you and beg ch at top; join yarn in first unused lp of beg ch; ch 1, sc in same lp; working in rem unused lps of beg ch, dc in next lp; *ch 17, 2 dc in 3rd ch from hook and in each of next 14 chs—*spiral made;* [sc in next lp, dc in next lp] twice; rep from * to last 2 lps; ch 17, 2 dc in 3rd ch from hook and in each of next 14 chs—*spiral made;* sc in next lp, dc in last lp.

Fasten off and weave in ends. ◆

Lullaby Luvie

Need a baby shower gift in a hurry? This quick-and-easy baby afghan is made with soft blue and white textured stripes.

DESIGN BY TIFFINEY KRUCEK

Skill Level
EASY

Finished Size
35 x 38 inches

Materials
- Caron Simply Soft medium (worsted) weight yarn (6 oz/330 yds/170g per skein): 3 skeins #9701 white, 2 skeins #9712 soft blue
- Size H/8/5mm crochet hook or size needed to obtain gauge
- Tapestry needle

Gauge
3 ch-3 sps = 2 inches; 3 ch sp rows = 1 inch

Pattern Notes
Weave in loose ends as work progresses.

Join rounds with a slip stitch unless otherwise stated.

Special Stitch
Cluster (cl): Yo, insert hook in indicated st, yo, draw up a lp, yo, draw through 2 lps on hook, (yo, insert hook in same sp, yo, draw up a lp, yo, draw through 2 lps on hook) 3 times, yo, draw through all 5 lps on hook.

Afghan
Row 1 (RS): With soft blue, ch 198, sc in 2nd ch from hook, [ch 3, sk next 3 chs, sc in next ch] across, turn. *(49 ch-3 sps)*

Row 2: Ch 4, sc in first ch-3 sp, [ch 3, sc in next ch-3 sp] across to include last ch-3 sp, ch 3, sc in the last sc on row, turn. *(50 ch-3 sps)*

Row 3: Sl st into the first ch-3 sp, ch 1, sc in same sp, [ch 3, sc in next ch-3 sp] across, turn. *(49 ch-3 sps)*

Rows 4–7: [Rep rows 2 and 3 alternately] twice. At the end of row 7, **change colour** *(see Stitch Guide, p. 31)* to white, turn.

Row 8: Ch 4, hdc in first ch-3 sp, (**cl**—*see Special Stitch*, hdc) in same sp, [ch 3, sc in next ch sp, ch 3, (hdc, cl, hdc) in next ch sp] across to include last ch-3 sp, ch 3, sc in last sc on row, turn. *(25 cls)*

Row 9: Rep row 3.

Row 10: Ch 4, sc in first ch-3 sp, [ch 3, (hdc, cl, hdc) in next ch sp, ch 3, sc in next ch sp] across to include last sp, ch 3, sc in last sc on row, turn. *(24 cls)*

Row 11: Rep row 3.

Row 12: Rep row 8. At the end of row 12 change colour to soft blue, turn.

Row 13: Rep row 3.

Rows 14–19: [Rep rows 2 and 3 alternately] 3 times. At the end of row 19 change colour to white, turn.

Row 20: Rep row 10.

Row 21: Rep row 3.

Row 22: Rep row 8.

Row 23: Rep row 3.

Row 24: Rep row 10. At the end of row 24 change colour to soft blue, turn.

Rows 25–31: Rep rows 13–19.

Rows 32–36: Rep rows 8–12.

Rows 37–43: Rep rows 13–19.

Rows 44–48: Rep rows 20–24.

Rows 49–55: Rep rows 13–19.

Rows 56–60: Rep rows 8–12.

Rows 61–67: Rep rows 13–19.

Rows 68–72: Rep rows 20–24.

Rows 73–79: Rep rows 13–19.

Rows 80–84: Rep rows 8–12.

Rows 85–91: Rep rows 13–19.

Rows 92–96: Rep rows 20–24.

Rows 97–103: Rep rows 13–19.

Rows 104–108: Rep rows 8–12.

Rows 109–115: Rep rows 13–19. At the end of row 115, fasten off soft blue.

CONTINUED ON PAGE 154

Naptime Shells

A sweet striped pattern of soft puffy shells in luscious lavender, yellow and white creates the precious design of this cozy, easy-to-stitch blanket.

DESIGN BY MELISSA LEAPMAN

Skill Level

EASY

Size

37 x 46 inches

Materials

- Patons Astra light (light worsted) weight yarn (1¾ oz/161 yds/50g per ball): 7 balls #02751 white *(A)*, 5 balls #02315 bright lilac *(B)*, 4 balls #02759 baby yellow*(C)*
- Size I/9/5.5mm crochet hook or size needed to obtain gauge
- Yarn needle

Gauge

[Sc, shell] 4 times = 7 inches; 5 rows = 3 inches
Check gauge to save time.

Pattern Notes

Weave in loose ends as work progresses.

Join rounds with a slip stitch unless otherwise stated.

Afghan

Foundation row (RS): With C, ch 130, 2 dc in 4th ch from hook, *sk next 2 chs, sc in next ch, sk next 2 chs **, 5 dc in next ch, rep from * across, ending last rep at **, 3 dc in last ch, change to A, turn. *(20 groups 5-dc; 21 sc; 2 groups 3-dc)*

Row 1 (WS): Ch 1, sc in first dc, *ch 3, **dc dec** (see Stitch Guide, p. 31) over next 5 sts, ch 3 **, sc in next dc, rep from * across, ending last rep at **, sc in top of beg ch-3, change to B, turn. *(21 groups dc dec)*

Row 2: Ch 3, 2 dc in first sc, *sk next ch-3 sp, sc into next dc dec, sk next ch-3 sp **, 5 dc into next sc, rep from * across, ending last rep at **, 3 dc in last sc, change to A, turn.

Row 3: Rep row 1, change to C, turn.

Row 4: Rep row 2, change to A, turn.

Rep rows 1–4 for pattern until afghan measures approximately 45½ inches, ending with a row 3 pattern, fasten off.

Border

Rnd 1 (RS): Attach B with sl st in any corner, ch 1, sc evenly spaced around outer edge, working 3 sc in each corner, join in beg sc.

Rnd 2 (RS): Ch 1, sc in each sc around, working 3 sc in each centre corner sc around, join in beg sc, fasten off. ✦

Giggles

Alternating rows of lacy and solid stitches look like strips in this sweet, one-piece design.

DESIGN BY DARLA SIMS

Skill Level

EASY

Finished Size
Approximately 37 x 42 inches

Materials
- Bernat Satin medium (worsted) weight yarn (3½ oz/163 yds/100g per ball): 5 balls #04423 flamingo (A), 2 balls #04005 snow (B)
- Bernat Baby Bubbles bulky (chunky) weight yarn (2½ oz/105 yds/70g per ball): 4 balls #75712 baby bubble pink (C)
- Sizes H/8/5mm and I/9/5.5mm crochet hooks or size needed to obtain gauge
- Tapestry needle

Gauge
Size I hook and medium yarn: 3 dc = 1 inch

Special Stitches
V-stitch (V-st): In st indicated work (dc, ch 1, dc).
Cluster (cl): Keeping last lp of each dc on hook, 2 dc in st indicated, yo and draw through all 3 lps on hook.

Centre
Row 1 (WS): With I hook and A, ch 112; dc in 4th ch from hook *(beg 3 sk chs count as a dc)* and in each rem ch, turn. *(110 dc)*
Row 2 (RS): Ch 3 *(counts as a dc on this and following rows)*, dc in each dc and in 3rd ch of beg 3 sk chs; change to B by drawing lp through; cut A, turn.
Row 3: Ch 4 *(counts as a dc and a ch-1 sp on this and following rows)*, sk next dc; *V-st *(see Special Stitches)* in next dc; sk next 2 dc; rep from * 34 times; V-st in next dc, sk next dc, dc in 3rd ch of turning ch-3; change to C by drawing lp through; cut B, turn. *(36 V-sts)*
Row 4: Ch 4; *cl *(see Special Stitches)* in ch-1 sp of next V-st; ch 2; rep from * 34 times; cl in ch-1 sp of next V-st; ch 1, dc in 3rd ch of turning ch-4; change to A; cut C, turn.
Row 5: Ch 3, dc in next ch-1 sp; *dc in next cl, 2 dc in next ch-2 sp; rep from * 34 times; dc in next cl, in sp formed by turning ch-4 and in 3rd ch of turning ch, turn.
Row 6: Ch 3, dc in each dc and in 3rd ch of turning ch-3; change to B; cut A, turn.
Rows 7–58: Rep rows 3–6 consecutively 13 times. At end of row 58, do not change colours.

Fasten off and weave in all ends.

Edging
Rnd 1 (RS): Hold Centre with RS facing you and 1 short end at top; with H hook, join B in first dc in upper right-hand corner; ch 1, 3 sc in same ch as joining—*corner made;* sc in each dc to turning ch-3; 3 sc in 3rd ch of turning ch-3—*corner made;* working across next side in ends of rows, sc evenly spaced to beg ch; working across next side in unused lps of beg ch, 3 sc in first lp—*corner made;* sc in each lp to last lp; 3 sc in last lp—*corner made;* working across next side in ends of rows, sc evenly spaced to first sc; join with sl st in first sc.
Rnd 2: Ch 3 *(counts as a dc on this and following rnd)*, 3 dc in next sc—*dc corner made;* *dc in each sc to 2nd sc of next corner; 3 dc in 2nd sc—*dc corner made;* rep from * twice; dc in each sc to beg ch-3; join with sl st in 3rd ch of beg ch-3; change to C; cut B. Turn.
Rnd 3: Ch 3; *dc in each dc to 2nd dc of next corner; dc corner in 2nd dc; rep from * 3 times; dc in next dc; join with sl st in 3rd ch of beg ch-3.
Fasten off and weave in all ends. ◆

Warm & Cuddly

A clever pattern combining front and back loop stitches gives this design a bobbled look.

DESIGN BY MARY ANN SIPES

Skill Level

EASY

Finished Size
Approximately 27 x 39 inches

Materials
- Red Heart Baby Clouds super bulky (super chunky)weight yarn (4½ oz/105 yds/127g per skein): 3 skeins #9832 blue swirl (A)
- Plymouth Baby Rimini super bulky (super chunky) weight yarn (1¾ oz/38 yds/50oz per ball): 8 balls #202 pastel yellow (B)
- Size M/13/9mm crochet hook or size needed to obtain gauge
- Tapestry needle

Gauge
4 sc = 2 inches

Pattern Note
To change colour, work last stitch until 2 loops remain on hook; with new colour, yarn over and draw through 2 loops on hook. Cut old colour.

Centre
Row 1 (RS): With A, ch 70; sc in 2nd ch from hook and in each rem ch, turn. (69 sc)
Row 2: Ch 1, working in **front** lps (see Stitch Guide, p. 31) only, sc in each sc, turn.
Row 3: Ch 1, sc in first sc; *dc in unused lp of next sc on row 1, sk next sc on working row behind dc just made, sc in next sc; rep from * across. (69 sts)
Row 4: Ch 1, working in front lps only, sc in each st, turn.
Row 5: Ch 1, sc in first sc; *dc in unused lp of next dc on row 3, sk next sc on working row behind dc just made, sc in next sc; rep from * across, turn.
Row 6: Rep row 4, changing to B in last sc, turn.
Row 7: Ch 1, sc in first sc; *dc in unused lp of next dc 1 row below, sk next sc on working row behind dc just made, sc in next sc; rep from * across, turn.
Row 8: Rep row 4.
Row 9: Ch 1, sc in first sc; *dc in unused lp of next dc 1 row below, sk next sc on working row behind dc just made, sc in next sc; rep from * across, turn.
Row 10: Rep row 4, changing to A in last sc, turn.
Row 11: Ch 1, sc in first sc; *dc in unused lp of next dc 1 row below, sk next sc on working row behind dc just made, sc in next sc; rep from * across, turn.
Row 12: Rep row 4.
Row 13: Ch 1, sc in first sc; *dc in unused lp of next dc 1 row below, sk next sc on working row behind sc just made, sc in next sc; rep from * across, turn.
Row 14: Rep row 4.
Rows 15–46: [Work rows 7–14 consecutively] 4 times.
Fasten off and weave in all ends.

Border
Rnd 1 (RS): Hold Centre with RS facing you and 1 short end at top; join B with sl st in first sc in upper right-hand corner; ch 1, 3 sc in same sc—corner made; sc in each sc to last sc; 3 sc in last sc—corner made; working across next side in ends of rows, sc in each row; working across next side in unused lps of beg ch, 3 sc in first lp—corner made; sc in each lp to last lp; 3 sc in last lp—corner made; working across next side in ends of rows, sc in each row; join with sl st in **back lp** (see Stitch Guide) only of first sc.
Rnd 2: Ch 1, sc in same lp as joining; working in back lps only, corner in next sc; *sc in each sc to 2nd sc of next corner; corner in 2nd sc; rep from * twice; sc in each sc to first sc; join with sl st in first sc.
Fasten off and weave in ends. ◆

Posies for Baby

These pretty posies are crocheted onto the blanket as you work, so there's no sewing!

DESIGN BY NANCY NEHRING

Skill Level

■ ■ □ □
EASY

Finished Size

Approximately 28 x 32 inches

Materials

- Red Heart Baby Clouds super bulky (super chunky) weight yarn (6 oz/140 yds/170g per skein): 3 skeins #9364 aqua (A)
- Red Heart Classic medium (worsted) weight yarn (3½ oz/190 yds/99g per skein): 2 skeins #737 pink (B)
- Sizes I/9/5.5mm and N/15/10mm crochet hooks or size needed to obtain gauge
- Tapestry needle
- Stitch holder

Gauge

Size N hook: 7 sc = 4 inches

Special Stitch

Cluster (cl): Keeping last lp of each dc on hook, 2 dc in st indicated, yo and draw through all 3 lps on hook.

Blanket

Row 1 (WS): With N hook and A, ch 44; sc in 2nd ch from hook and in each rem ch, turn. (43 sc)

Row 2 (RS): Ch 1, sc in each sc, turn.

Rows 3 & 4: Rep row 2. At end of row 4, drop A.

Note: Place stitch holder in last sc of last row. Due to the light yarn weight of B, when working sc on the following row, pull horizontal lp of sc to span distance from 1 sc of previous row to next sc. This prevents previous row from bunching.

Row 5: Hold piece with RS facing you; with I hook, join B with sl st in first sc of previous row; ch 1, sc in same sc as joining and in next 2 sc; ch 4; join with sl st in first ch to form ring; turn ring only; in ring work [sl st, hdc, dc, hdc] 3 times—3 petals made; insert hook in ring and in 2nd sc of beg 3 sc made, draw lp though; in ring work (hdc, dc, hdc)—petal made; in ring work (sl st, hdc, dc, hdc)—petal made; join with sl st in first sl st in ring—flower made; sc in next 6 sc of previous row; *ch 4; join with sl st in first ch to form ring; turn ring only; in ring work [sl st, hdc, dc, hdc] 3 times—3 petals made; insert hook in ring and in 2nd sc of previous 6 sc made, draw lp though; in ring work (hdc, dc, hdc)—petal made; in ring work (sl st, hdc,

dc, hdc)—petal made; join with sl st in first sl st in ring—flower made; sc in next 6 sc of previous row; rep from * 4 times; ch 4; join with sl st in first ch to form ring; turn ring only; in ring work [sl st, hdc, dc, hdc] 3 times—3 petals made; insert hook in ring and in 2nd sc of previous 6 sc made, draw lp though; in ring work (hdc, dc, hdc)—petal made; in ring work (sl st, hdc, dc, hdc)—petal made; join with sl st in first sl st in ring—flower made; sc in last 3 sc of previous row, turn. (7 flowers)

Note: Change to N hook and pick up A; fasten off B.

Row 6: Ch 1, working over sc of previous row and keeping flowers to back of work, sc in each sc on 2nd row below, turn.

Rows 7–9: Rep row 2.

Note: Place stitch holder in last sc of last row.

Row 10: Hold piece with RS facing you; with I hook, join B with sl st in first sc of previous row; ch 1, sc in same sc as joining and in next 6 sc; ch 4, join to form ring; turn ring only; in ring work [sl st, hdc, dc, hdc] 3 times—3 petals made; insert hook in ring and in 2nd sc of beg

CONTINUED ON PAGE 154

Spring Bouquet Baby Afghan

Soft pastel baby yarns gives life to an adorable baby blanket, complemented with yellow and pink flowers.

DESIGN BY MICHELLE CREAN

Skill Level

EASY

Finished Size

33 x 45 inches

Materials

- Baby pompadour super fine (fingering) weight yarn: 8¾ oz/1295 yds/ 248g white, 3 oz/518 yds/85g each pink and yellow, 1¾ oz/ 259 yds/50g green
- Size D/3/3.25mm crochet hook or size needed to obtain gauge
- Tapestry needle

Gauge

Motif = 6 inches square

Pattern Notes

Weave in loose ends as work progresses.

Join rounds with a slip stitch unless otherwise stated.

Special Stitches

Beginning double crochet (beg dc): Sc, ch 2.
Front post single crochet (fpsc):

Insert hook front to back to front again around the vertical post of indicated st, yo, draw up a lp, yo, draw through 2 lps on hook.
Picot: Ch 3, sc in top of previous st.
Corner shell: (3 dc, ch 2, 3 dc) in indicated st.
Beginning corner shell (beg corner shell): (Beg dc, 2 dc, ch 2, 3 dc) in indicated st.
Border shell: 5 dc in indicated st.

Motif

Make 18 flowers with A.
Make 17 flowers with B.
Rnd 1: With A (B), ch 3, sl st to join in first ch to form a ring, ch 1, [sc in ring, ch 2] 8 times, join in beg sc. *(8 ch-2 sps)*
Rnd 2: Ch 1, [sc, ch 1, hdc, ch 1, sc] in each ch-2 sp around, join in beg sc, turn. *(8 petals)*
Rnd 3: Ch 1, [**fpsc** *(see Special Stitches)* around next sc of rnd 1 directly below, ch 2] 8 times, join in beg sc, turn.
Rnd 4: Ch 1, [sc, ch 1, {hdc, ch 1} twice, sc] in each ch-2 sp around, join in beg sc, turn.

Rnd 5: Ch 1, working around posts of sc of rnd 3, [fpsc around next sc, ch 3] 8 times, join in beg sc, turn.
Rnd 6: Ch 1, [sc, ch 1, (hdc, ch 1) 3 times, sc] in each ch-3 sp around, join in beg sc, fasten off.
Rnd 7: Working in **back lp** *(see Stitch Guide, p. 31)* of each st, attach green in centre hdc of any petal, **beg dc** *(see Special Stitches)*, (2 dc, ch 2, 3 dc) in same st as beg dc for corner, ch 1, sk 3 sts of next petal, working in centre 3 st of next petal, sc in ch between first 2 hdc, sc in centre hdc of petal, sc in next ch, ch 1, [**corner shell** *(see Special Stitches)* in centre hdc of next petal, ch 1, working in centre 3 sts of next petal, sc in ch between first 2 hdc, sc in centre hdc of petal, sc in next ch, ch 1] 3 times, join in beg sc, fasten off. *(4 corner shells, 8 ch-1 sps, 12 sc)*
Rnd 8: Attach white in any corner ch-2 sp, **beg corner shell** *(see Special Stitches)* in corner ch-2 sp, ch 1, 3 dc in next ch-1 sp, ch 1, sk next 3 sc, 3 dc in next ch-1 sp, ch 1, [corner shell

in next ch-2 sp of corner, ch 1, 3 dc in next ch-1 sp, ch 1, 3 dc in next ch-1 sp, ch 1] 3 times, join in top of beg dc, fasten off. *(12 dc between each corner ch-2 sp)*

Rnd 9: Attach B (A) in any corner ch-2 sp, beg corner shell in same ch-2 sp, *ch 1, [3 dc in next ch-1 sp, ch 1] 3 times**, corner shell in next ch-2 sp, rep from * around, ending last rep at **, join in top of beg dc, fasten off.

Rnd 10: Attach white in any corner ch-2 sp, beg corner shell in same ch-2 sp, *ch 1, [3 dc in next ch-1 sp, ch 1] 4 times**, corner shell in next corner ch-2 sp, rep from * around, ending last rep at **, **do not join.** *(18 dc between corner ch-2 sps)*

Rnd 11: Beg dc in next dc, dc in each dc to corner *(2 dc, ch 2, 2 dc) in corner ch-2 sp, dc in each dc and each ch to next corner ch-2 sp, rep from * around. *(27 dc between corner ch-2 sps)*

Rnd 12: [Sc in each dc across to corner ch-2 sp, 3 sc in corner ch-2 sp] around, join in beg sc, fasten off. *(120 sc)*

Assembly

With white yarn and tapestry needle, with RS facing and alternating colours as indicated, sew Motifs tog from centre of corner through both lps of sts to opposite corner.
Sew 7 strips of 5 motifs each and sew strips tog.

```
A B A B A
B A B A B
A B A B A
B A B A B
A B A B A
B A B A B
A B A B A
```

Edging

Rnd 1: Attach white in any centre corner sc, ch 1, [{sc, ch 2, sc} in centre corner sc, sc in each sc across, including block corners on either side of seams] 4 times, join in beg sc.

Rnd 2: Ch 1, *(sc, ch 2, sc) in corner ch-2 sp, ch 1, sc in next sc, [ch 1, sk next sc, sc in next sc] across to corner ch-2 sp, ch 1, rep from * around, join in beg sc, fasten off.

Rnd 3: Attach A in any corner ch-2 sp, ch 1, *(sc, ch 2, sc) in corner ch-2 sp, [ch 1, sk next sc, sc in next ch-1 sp] across to corner ch-2 sp, ch 1, rep from * around, join in beg sc, fasten off.

Rnd 4: Attach white, rep rnd 3.

Rnd 5: Attach green, rep rnd 3.

Rnd 6: Attach white, rep rnd 3.

Do not fasten off.

Rnd 7: Working in ch sps and sk sc sts, ch 1, working across long side, (beg dc, 4 dc) in corner sp, sc in next ch-1 sp [**border shell** *(see Special Stitches, p. 116)* in next ch-1 sp, sk next ch-1 sp, sc in next ch-1 sp] 37 times, border shell in next ch-1 sp, sc in last ch-1 sp, border shell in corner ch-2 sp, working across short side, sc in next ch-1 sp, sk next ch-1 sp, [border shell in next ch-1 sp, sk next ch-1 sp, sc in next ch-1 sp] across, border shell in corner ch-2 sp, working across long side, sc in next ch-1 sp, [border shell in next ch-1 sp, sk next ch-1 sp, sc in next ch-1 sp] 37 times, border shell in next ch-1 sp, sc in last ch-1 sp, border shell in corner sp, working across short side, sc in next ch-1 sp, sk next ch-1 sp, [border shell in next ch-1 sp, sk next ch-1 sp, sc in next ch-1 sp] across, join in top of beg dc, fasten off.

Rnd 8: Attach B in first dc of any border shell worked in a corner ch-2 sp, ch 1, *sc in first dc of border shell, [ch 1, sc in next dc] 4 times, sk next sc, rep from * around, join in beg sc, fasten off.

Rnd 9: Attach white in first ch-1 sp of any border shell worked in a corner, ch 1, *sc in first ch-1 sp of border shell, [ch 2, sc in next ch-1 sp] 3 times, sk next 2 sc, rep from * around, join in beg sc.

Note: *Work in ch-2 sps only, except on either side of corners as directed.*

Rnd 10: Ch 1, sc, **picot** *(see Special Stitches)* in next ch-2 sp, (sc, picot) in next 2 ch-2 sps, (sc, picot) between next 2 sc, (sc, picot) in each ch-2 sp across to border shell at corner, *[{sc, picot} between next 2 sc, {sc, picot} in next 3 ch-2 sps, {sc, picot} between next 2 sc] for border shell at corner, (sc, picot) in each ch-2 sp across side, rep from * 3 times, ending with (sc, picot) between last 2 sc, join in first sc, fasten off. ◆

Grandma's Double Delight

Five colours worked in six different arrangements give fun variety to the motifs in this charming blanket.

DESIGN BY ELAINE BARTLETT

Skill Level

EASY

Finished Size

Approximately 30 x 36 inches

Materials

- Red Heart Super Saver medium (worsted) weight yarn (7 oz/364 yds/198g per skein): 2 skeins #311 white (A), 1 skein each #381 light blue (B), #724 baby pink (C), #322 pale yellow (D), #363 pale green (E)
- Size I/9/5.5mm crochet hook or size needed to obtain gauge
- Tapestry needle

Gauge

Motif = 4½ x 4½ inches

Motif

Make 7 each of Motifs A-F.

Note: *See Motif Chart for colour sequence.*

Rnd 1 (RS): With A, ch 4; join with sl st to form ring; ch 3 *(counts as a dc)*, 2 dc in ring; ch 2, in ring work [3 dc, ch 2] 3 times; join with sl st in first sc. Fasten off. *(12 dc)*

Rnd 2: With 2nd colour, make slip knot on hook and join with sc in **back lp** (see Stitch Guide, p. 31) only of first dc of any 3-dc group; sc in back lp of next 2 dc; *3 sc in next ch-2 sp—*corner made;* sc in back lp of next 3 dc; rep from * twice; 3 sc in next ch-2 sp—*corner made;* join with sl st in first sc. Fasten off. *(24 sc)*

Rnd 3: With 3rd colour, make slip knot on hook and join with sc in back lp of 3rd sc of any corner; *[dc in unused **front lp** (see Stitch

Guide) of next dc on rnd 1; sk next sc on working rnd behind dc just made, sc in back lp of next sc] twice; corner in next sc; sc in back lp of next sc; rep from * twice; [dc in unused front lp of next dc on rnd 1, sk next sc on working rnd behind dc just made, sc in back lp of next sc] twice; corner in next sc; join with sl st in first sc. Fasten off. *(32 sts)*

Rnd 4: With 4th colour, make slip knot on hook and join with sc in back lp of 3rd sc of any corner; *[dc in unused front lp of next st 1 rnd below, sk next st on working rnd behind dc just made, sc in back lp of next st] 3 times; corner in next sc; sc in back lp of next st; rep from * twice; [dc in unused front lp of next st 1 rnd below,

Motif Chart

Motif	Rnd 1	Rnd 2	Rnd 3	Rnd 4	Rnd 5	Rnds 6 & 7
A	white	yellow	pink	blue	green	white
B	white	green	yellow	blue	pink	white
C	white	pink	blue	green	yellow	white
D	white	yellow	green	pink	blue	white
E	white	blue	pink	yellow	green	white
F	white	green	blue	pink	yellow	white

Motif Chart

Assembly Diagram

A	B	C	D	E	F
B	C	D	E	F	A
C	D	E	F	A	B
D	E	F	A	B	C
E	F	A	B	C	D
F	A	B	C	D	E
A	B	C	D	E	F

Assembly Diagram

sk next st on working rnd behind dc just made, sc in back lp of next st] 3 times; corner in next sc; join with sl st in joining sc. Fasten off. *(40 sts)*

Rnd 5: With 5th colour, make slip knot on hook and join with sc in back lp of 3rd sc of any corner; *[dc in unused front lp of next st 1 rnd below, sk next sc on working rnd behind dc just made, sc in back lp of next sc] 4 times; corner in next sc; sc in back lp of next sc; rep from * twice; [dc in unused front lp of next st 1 rnd below, sk next sc on working rnd behind dc just made, sc in back lp of next sc] 4 times; corner in next sc; join with sl st in joining sc. Fasten off. *(48 sts)*

Rnd 6: With A, make slip knot on hook and join with sc in back lp of 3rd sc of any corner; *[dc in unused front lp of next st 1 rnd below, sk next sc on working rnd behind dc just made, sc in back lp of next sc] 5 times; corner in next sc; sc in back lp of next sc; rep from * twice; [dc in unused front lp of next st 1 rnd below, sk next sc on working rnd behind dc just made, sc in back lp of next sc] 5 times; corner in next sc; join in joining sc. *(56 sts)*

Rnd 7: Ch 1, hdc in same sc as joining; *sc in next 9 sts, hdc in next 2 sts, 3 dc in centre sc of corner**, hdc in next 2 sts, rep from * twice; ending at ** on last rep, hdc in last st; join with sl st in first hdc. *(64 sts)*
Fasten off and weave in all ends.

Assembly

Following Assembly Diagram for colour placement, join Motifs in 7 rows of 6 Motifs each. To join Motifs, hold 2 Motifs with WS tog; with tapestry needle and A and working in back lps only, sew Motifs tog, beg and ending in 2nd dc of corners. Secure corners by working in both lps of each corner st.

Edging

Rnd 1 (RS): Hold piece with RS facing you and 1 short end at top; with A make slip knot on hook and join with sc in 3rd dc of upper right-hand corner; sc in next 14 sts; ***hdc dec** (see Stitch Guide, p. 31)* in next 2 joined dc; sc in next 15 sts; rep from * to 2nd dc on next outer corner; 3 sc in 2nd dc—*corner made*; sc in next 15 sts; **hdc dec in next 2 joined dc; sc in next 15 sts; rep from ** to 2nd dc on next outer corner; 3 sc in 2nd dc—*corner made*; sc in next 15 sts, ***hdc dec in next 2 joined dc; sc in next 15 sts; rep from *** to 2nd dc on next outer corner; 3 sc in 2nd dc—*corner made*; sc in next 15 sts, ****hdc dec in next 2 joined dc; sc in next 15 sts; rep from **** to 2nd dc on next outer corner; 3 sc in 2nd dc—*corner made*; join with sl st in first hdc. Fasten off.

Rnd 2: With B, make slip knot on hook and join with sc in 2nd sc of any corner; 2 sc in same sc; *working in back lps only, sc in each sc to 2nd sc of next corner; working through both lps of sc, corner in 2nd sc; rep from * twice; working in back lps only, sc in each sc to first sc; join with sl st in joining sc. Fasten off.

Rnd 3: With C, make slip knot on hook and join with sc in back lp of 3rd sc of any corner; *dc in unused front lp of next sc 1 rnd below, sk next sc on working rnd behind dc just made, sc in back lp of next sc; rep from * to 2nd sc of next corner; working through both lps of sc, corner in 2nd sc; sc in back lp of next sc, **dc in unused front lp of next sc 1 rnd below, sk next sc on working rnd behind dc just made, sc in back lp of next sc; rep from ** to 2nd sc of next corner; working through both lps of sc, corner in 2nd sc; sc in back lp of next sc, ***dc in unused front lp of next sc 1 rnd below, sk next sc on working rnd behind dc just made, sc in back lp of next sc; rep from *** to 2nd sc of next corner; working through both lps of sc, corner in 2nd sc; sc in back lp of next sc, ****dc in unused front lp of next sc 1 rnd below, sk next sc on working rnd behind dc just made, sc in back lp of next sc; rep from **** to 2nd sc of next corner; working through both lps of sc, corner in 2nd sc; join with sl st in joining sc. Fasten off.

Rnd 4: With D, rep rnd 3.

Rnd 5: With E, rep rnd 3.

Rnd 6: With A, rep rnd 3. At end of rnd, do not fasten off.

Rnd 7: Ch 1, hdc in same sc as joining; *sc in each st to last 2 sts before 2nd sc of next corner, hdc in next 2 sts, 3 dc in 2nd sc of corner; hdc in next 2 sts, rep from * twice; sc in each st to last 2 sts before 2nd sc of next corner; hdc in next 2 sts, 3 dc in 2nd sc of corner; hdc in next st; join in first hdc.
Fasten off and weave in all ends. ✦

A Patchwork Blue

Rows of alternating-colour stitches combined with surface chains create a this pretty patchwork.

DESIGN BY RENA V. STEVENS

Skill Level
■■□□
EASY

Size
46 x 51 inches

Materials
- Red Heart Sport light (sport) weight yarn (2½ oz/165 yds/70g per skein): 10 skeins #819 blue jewel, 5 skeins #1 white
- Sizes G/6/4mm and J/10/6mm crochet hooks or size needed to obtain gauge
- Yarn needle

Gauge
Size G hook: 4 dc = 1 inch; 6 dc rows = 2½ inches

Pattern Notes
Weave in loose ends as work progresses.

Join rounds with a slip stitch unless otherwise stated.

Make colour change by using new colour to complete last step of last stitch made in old colour, fasten off old colour.

Afghan
Row 1 (RS): With size G hook and blue jewel, ch 147, dc in 5th ch from hook, dc in each of next 102 chs, [ch 2 loosely, sk next 2 chs, dc in each of next 2 chs] 10 times, turn.

Row 2: With white, ch 2 (counts as first dc throughout), dc in next dc, [ch 2 loosely, sk next 2 chs, dc in each of next 2 dc] 10 times, **change colour** (see Stitch Guide, p. 31) to blue jewel, dc in each rem dc across, turn.

Row 3: Ch 2, dc in each of next 103 dc, [ch 2 loosely, sk next 2 chs, dc in each of next 2 dc] 10 times, turn.

Rows 4–20: [Rep rows 2 and 3 alternately] 9 times, ending last rep with row 2, **do not turn**.

Row 21 (WS): Attach blue jewel with a sl st in top of beg ch-2, dc in next dc, [2 dc in next ch-2 sp, dc in each of next 2 dc] 10 times, with white, dc in each of next 34 dc, [ch 2 loosely, sk next 2 dc, dc in each of next 2 dc] across to end of row, turn.

Row 22: With blue jewel, ch 2, dc in next dc, [ch 2 loosely, sk next ch-2 sp, dc in each of next 2 dc] 16 times, ch 2 loosely, sk next ch-2 sp, dc in each rem dc across, turn.

Rnd 23: Ch 2, dc in each of next 41 dc, join white in last step of last dc made, fasten off blue jewel, dc in each of next 34 dc, [ch 2 loosely, sk next ch-2 sp, dc in each of next 2 dc] across, turn.

Rows 24–35: [Rep rows 22 and 23 alternately] 6 times.

Row 36 (RS): With blue jewel, ch 2, dc in next dc, [2 dc in next ch-2 sp, dc in each of next 2 dc] 16 times, 2 dc in next ch-2 sp, dc in each rem dc across, turn.

Row 37: Ch 2, dc in each of next 41 dc, with white, dc in each of next 34 dc, with blue jewel, dc in each rem dc across, turn.

Row 38: Ch 2, dc in each dc across, turn.

Rows 39–56: [Rep rows 37 and 38 alternately] 9 times.

Row 57 (WS): Ch 2, dc in each of next 41 dc, with white, [dc in each of next 2 dc, ch 2 loosely, sk next 2 dc] 18 times, dc in each rem dc across, turn.

Row 58: With blue jewel, ch 2, dc in each of next 29 dc, [ch 2 loosely, sk next 2 chs, dc in each of next 2 dc] 18 times, dc in each rem dc across, turn.

Row 59: Ch 2, dc in each of next 41 dc, with white, [dc in each of next 2 dc, ch 2 loosely, sk next 2 chs] 18 times, dc in each rem dc across, turn.

Rows 60–71: [Rep rows 58 and 59 alternately] 6 times.

Row 72 (RS): Rep row 58.

Row 73: Ch 2, dc in each of next 41 dc, with white, [dc in each of next 2 dc, ch 2 loosely, sk next 2 chs] 18 times, with blue jewel, dc in each rem dc across, turn.

Rows 74–79: [Rep rows 72 and 73 alternately] 3 times, fasten off blue jewel, **do not turn**.

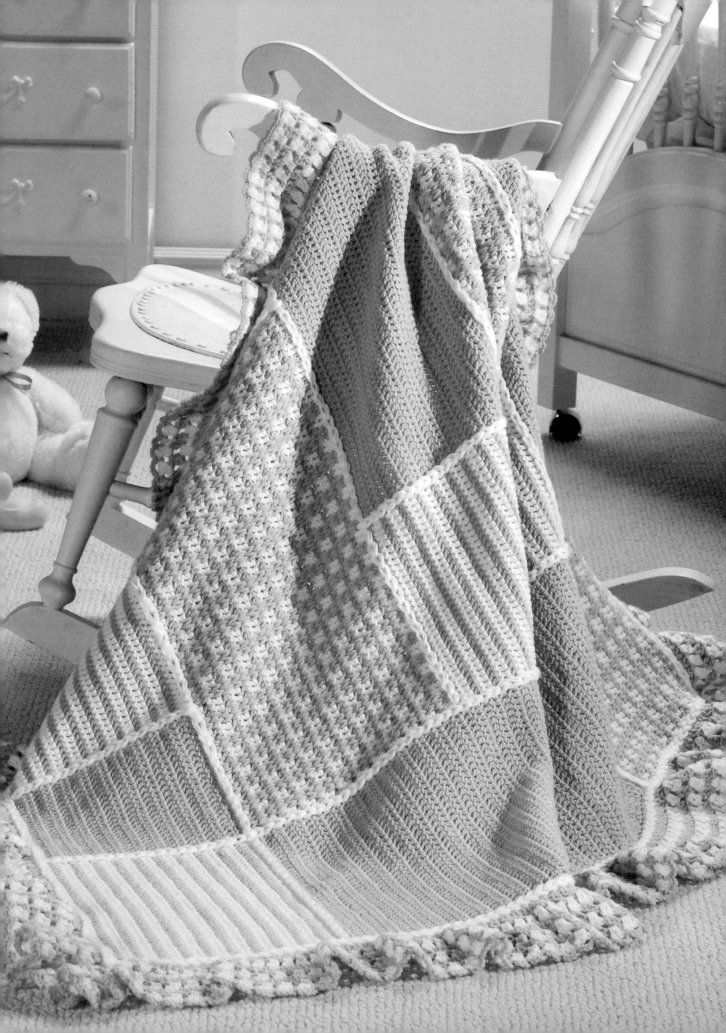

Row 80 (WS): Attach white with sl st in top of beg ch-2, dc in each of next 41 dc, with blue jewel, [dc in each of next 2 dc, 2 dc in next ch-2 sp] 6 times, dc in each of next 2 dc, with white, [2 dc in next ch-2 sp, dc in each of next 2 dc] 11 times, dc in each of next 2 dc, with blue jewel, dc in each dc across, turn.

Row 81 (RS): Ch 2, dc in each dc across, turn.

Row 82: With white, ch 2, dc in each of next 41 dc, with blue jewel, dc in each of next 26 dc, with white, dc in each of next 46 dc, with blue jewel, dc in each rem dc across, turn.

Rows 83–99: [Rep rows 81 and 82 alternately] 9 times, ending last rep with row 81, fasten off.

Finishing Checkered Patches

With hook size J and blue jewel, work 2 surface ch stripes vertically side by side in each ch-2 sp column, filling all ch-2 sps throughout afghan as follows: bottom left corner patch, with lp on hook, holding yarn beneath work and working on RS, sl st loosely over first row and into each ch sp to top of patch, draw up a lp in last ch sp, drop lp from hook, insert hook from underneath work to RS through bottom of next rows dc, draw lp through to back of work, ch 2 on WS of work to secure, fasten off.

For rem checkered patches, work same as previous except start each ch stripe by pulling lp from beneath work up through top of dc of the row below the current patch.

Trimming Patch Outlines

Working in similar manner as checkered patches using 2 strands of white held tog throughout, work a single surface ch stripe around edges of patches as follows: horizontal chs are worked with a sl st into every 2nd dc or sl st of each row bordering each patch.

Vertical chs are worked with a sl st into every row between dc sts bordering each patch.

Ruffled Edging

***Note:** Rnd 1 will pucker afghan edges.*

Rnd 1: With RS facing and starting at bottom right corner to work up right edge, with G hook, attach white with sl st in ch sp at end of first row, ch 3 *(counts as first dc throughout)*, working around posts of sts at ends of rows, dc around each st to next corner, ({dc, ch 1} 3 times, dc) around last st for corner, working normally into dc sts, *[sk next st, dc in each of next 2 sts, sk next st, dc in next st] across, ending last rep with sk next dc, dc in each of next 2 sts*, work corner st at edge of same row, dc in each st to next corner, rep corner around last st, working over opposite side of foundation ch, rep from * to *, (dc, ch 1) 3 times in same st as beg sl st, join in 3rd ch of beg ch-3, fasten off.

Rnd 2 (RS): Working in sps between posts of rnd 1 sts with 2 strands of yarns as follows: with size J hook, attach 2 strands of white with sl st in next sp, sl st loosely in each sp around, draw lp of last sl st made through beg sl st and fasten off on WS.

Rnd 3 (RS): Working in rnd 1 sts, with size G hook, attach blue jewel with sl st in first dc after rnd 1 beg ch-3, ch 3, dc in same dc, *[ch 1, 2 dc in next dc] across through first dc of next corner, (ch 2, 2 dc) in each of next 3 corner dc sts, rep from * around, ending with ch 1, sl st in top of beg ch-3, turn.

Rnd 4 (WS): With white, sl st in first ch-1 sp, ch 3, dc in same sp, ch 1, *({shell of 2 dc, ch 1, 2 dc}, ch 1) in each of next 3 corner sps, [2 dc in next ch sp, ch 1] across edge, rep from * around, join in 3rd ch of beg ch-3, turn.

Rnd 5 (RS): With blue jewel, sl st in next ch sp, ch 3, dc in same sp, ch 1, *[2 dc in next ch sp, ch 1] across to next corner shell, [shell in next ch-1 sp on next shell, ch 1, 2 dc in next ch-1 sp, ch 1] 3 times, rep from * around, join in 3rd ch of beg ch-3, turn.

Rnd 6 (WS): With white, sl st in first ch-1 sp, ch 3, dc in same sp, ch 1, 2 dc in next ch sp, *[ch 1, shell in next shell ch sp, {ch 1, 2 dc in next ch sp} twice] 3 times, [ch 1, 2 dc in next ch sp] across side edge, rep from * around, join in 3rd ch of beg ch-3, turn.

Rnd 7 (RS): With blue jewel, sl st in next ch sp, ch 3, dc in same ch sp, *[ch 1, 2 dc in next ch sp] across to next corner shell, [ch 1, shell in ch-1 sp of shell, {ch 1, 2 dc in next ch sp} 3 times] 3 times, rep from * around, ending after working last shell with, [ch 1, 2 dc in next ch sp] twice, ch 1, join in 3rd ch of beg ch-3, turn.

Rnd 8 (WS): With white, sl st in next ch sp, ch 3, dc in same sp, [ch 1, 2 dc in next ch sp] twice, *[ch 1, shell in next ch-1 sp of next shell, {ch 1, 2 dc in next ch sp} 4 times] 3 times, [ch 1, 2 dc in next ch sp] across, rep from * around, join in 3rd ch of beg ch-3, turn.

Rnd 9 (RS): With blue jewel, [sl st in next ch sp, ch 4] around, join in beg sl st, fasten off. ◆

Baby Burrito Blanket

With its circular design, this unique blanket makes it quick and easy to bundle up baby.

DESIGN BY CINDY ADAMS

Skill Level

EASY

Finished Size

Approximately 36 inches in diameter

Materials

- Red Heart Baby Econo medium (worsted) weight yarn (6 oz/460 yds/170g per skein): 2 skeins #1984 citrus multi
- Size G/6/4mm crochet hook or size needed to obtain gauge
- Tapestry needle

Gauge

Rnds 1–3 = 4 inches

Special Stitches

Beginning cluster (beg cl): Ch 2, [yo, draw up lp in sp indicated, yo, draw through 2 lps on hook] twice; yo and draw through all 3 lps on hook.

Cluster (cl): [Yo, draw up lp in sp indicated, yo, draw through 2 lps on hook] 3 times; yo and draw through all 4 lps on hook.

Blanket

Rnd 1 (RS): Ch 5, dc in 5th ch from hook *(beg 4 sk chs count as a dc and a ch-1 sp)*, ch 1, in same ch work [dc, ch 1] 6 times; join with sl st in 4th ch of beg 4 sk chs. *(8 ch-1 sps)*

Rnd 2: Sl st in next ch-1 sp; **beg cl** *(see Special Stitches)* in same sp, ch 2, *cl *(see Special Stitches)* in next ch-1 sp, ch 2; rep from * around; join with sl st in top of beg cl.

Rnd 3: Sl st in next ch-2 sp, in same sp work (beg cl, ch 2, cl); ch 2, in each rem ch-2 sp work (cl, ch2) twice; join with sl st in top of beg cl. *(16 ch-2 sps)*

Rnd 4: Sl st in next ch-2 sp, in same sp work (beg cl, ch 2, cl); ch 2, cl in next ch-2 sp, ch 2; *in next ch-2 sp work (cl, ch2) twice; cl in next ch-2 sp, ch 2; rep from * around; join with sl st in top of beg cl. *(24 ch-2 sps)*

Rnd 5: Sl st in next ch-2 sp, beg cl in same sp; ch 2, cl in next ch-2 sp; ch 2, in next ch-2 sp work (cl, ch2) twice; *[cl in next ch-2 sp, ch 2] twice; in next ch-2 sp work (cl, ch2) twice; rep from * around; join with sl st in top of beg cl. *(32 ch-2 sps)*

Rnd 6: Sl st in next ch-2 sp, beg cl in same sp; ch 2, [cl in next ch-2 sp, ch 2] 6 times; in next ch-2 sp work (cl, ch2) twice; *[cl in next ch-2 sp, ch 2] 7 times; in next ch-2 sp work (cl, ch2) twice; rep from * around; join with sl st in top of beg cl. *(36 ch-2 sps)*

Rnd 7: Sl st in next ch-2 sp, beg cl in same sp; ch 2, [cl in next ch-2 sp, ch 2] 4 times; in next ch-2 sp work (cl, ch2) twice; * [cl in next ch-2 sp, ch 2] 8 times; in next ch-2 sp work (cl, ch2) twice; rep from * twice, [cl in next ch-2 sp, ch 2] 3 times; join with sl st in top of beg cl. *(40 ch-2 sps)*

Rnd 8: Sl st in next ch-2 sp, in same sp work (beg cl, ch 2, cl); ch 2, [cl in next ch-2 sp, ch 2] 9 times; *in next ch-2 sp work (cl, ch2) twice; [cl in next ch-2 sp, ch 2] 9 times; rep from * around; join with sl st in top of beg cl. *(44 ch-2 sps)*

Rnd 9: Sl st in next ch-2 sp, beg cl in same sp; ch 2, [cl in next ch-2 sp, ch 2] 5 times; in next ch-2 sp work (cl, ch2) twice; *[cl in next ch-2 sp, ch 2] 10 times; in next ch-2 sp work (cl, ch2) twice; rep from * twice; [cl in next ch-2 sp, ch 2] 4 times; join with sl st in top of beg cl. *(48 ch-2 sps)*

Rnd 10: Sl st in next ch-2 sp, in same sp work (beg cl, ch 2, cl); ch 2, [cl in next ch-2 sp, ch 2] 11 times; *in next ch-2 sp work (cl, ch2) twice; [cl in next ch-2 sp, ch 2] 11 times; rep from * around; join with sl st in top of beg cl. *(52 ch-2 sps)*

Rnd 11: Sl st in next ch-2 sp, beg cl in same sp, ch 2, [cl in next ch-2 sp, ch 2] 5 times; in next ch-2 sp work (cl, ch2) twice; *[cl in next ch-2 sp, ch 2] 12 times; in next ch-2 sp work (cl, ch2) twice; rep from * twice; [cl in next ch-2 sp, ch 2] 6 times; join with sl st in top of beg cl. *(56 ch-2 sps)*

Rnd 12: Sl st in next ch-2 sp, in same sp work (beg cl, ch 2, cl); ch 2, [cl in next ch-2 sp, ch 2] 13 times; *in next ch-2 sp work (cl, ch2) twice; [cl in next ch-2 sp, ch 2] 13 times; rep from * around; join with sl st in top of beg cl. *(60 ch-2 sps)*

Rnd 13: Sl st in next ch-2 sp, beg cl in same sp; ch 2, [cl in next ch-2 sp, ch 2] 5 times; in next ch-2 sp work (cl, ch2) twice; *[cl in next ch-2 sp, ch 2] 14 times; in next ch-2 sp work (cl, ch2) twice; rep from * twice; [cl in next ch-2 sp,

ch 2] 8 times; join with sl st in top of beg cl. *(64 ch-2 sps)*

Rnd 14: Sl st in next ch-2 sp, in same sp work (beg cl, ch 2, cl); ch 2, [cl in next ch-2 sp, ch 2] 15 times; *in next ch-2 sp work (cl, ch2) twice; [cl in next ch-2 sp, ch 2] 15 times; rep from * around; join with sl st in top of beg cl. *(68 ch-2 sps)*

Rnd 15: Sl st in next ch-2 sp, beg cl in same sp, ch 2, [cl in next ch-2 sp, ch 2] 5 times; in next ch-2 sp work (cl, ch2) twice; *[cl in next ch-2 sp, ch 2] 16 times; in next ch-2 sp work (cl, ch2) twice; rep from * twice; [cl in next ch-2 sp, ch 2] 10 times; join with sl st in top of beg cl. *(72 ch-2 sps)*

Rnd 16: Sl st in next ch-2 sp, in same sp work (beg cl, ch 2, cl); ch 2, [cl in next ch-2 sp, ch 2] 8 times; *in next ch-2 sp work (cl, ch2) twice; [cl in next ch-2 sp, ch 2] 8 times; rep from * around; join with sl st in top of beg cl. *(80 ch-2 sps)*

Rnd 17: Sl st in next ch-2 sp, beg cl in same sp, ch 2, [cl in next ch-2 sp, ch 2] 3 times; in next ch-2 sp work (cl, ch2) twice; *[cl in next ch-2 sp, ch 2] 9 times; in next ch-2 sp work (cl, ch2) twice; rep from * 6 times; [cl in next ch-2 sp, ch 2] 5 times; join with sl st in top of beg cl. *(88 ch-2 sps)*

Rnd 18: Sl st in next ch-2 sp, in same sp work (beg cl, ch 2, cl); ch 2, [cl in next ch-2 sp, ch 2] 10 times; *in next ch-2 sp work (cl, ch2) twice; [cl in next ch-2 sp, ch 2] 10 times; rep from * around; join with sl st in top of beg cl. *(96 ch-2 sps)*

Rnd 19: Sl st in next ch-2 sp, beg cl in same sp; ch 2, [cl in next ch-2 sp, ch 2] 3 times; in next ch-2 sp work (cl, ch2) twice; *[cl in next ch-2 sp, ch 2] 11 times; in next

ch-2 sp work (cl, ch2) twice; rep from * 6 times; [cl in next ch-2 sp, ch 2] 7 times; join with sl st in top of beg cl. *(104 ch-2 sps)*

Rnd 20: Sl st in next ch-2 sp, in same sp work (beg cl, ch 2, cl); ch 2, [cl in next ch-2 sp, ch 2] 12 times; *in next ch-2 sp work (cl, ch2) twice; [cl in next ch-2 sp, ch 2] 12 times; rep from * around; join with sl st in top of beg cl. *(112 ch-2 sps)*

Rnd 21: Sl st in next ch-2 sp, beg cl in same sp, ch 2, [cl in next ch-2 sp, ch 2] twice; in next ch-2 sp work (cl, ch2) twice; *[cl in next ch-2 sp, ch 2] 6 times; in next ch-2 sp work (cl, ch2) twice; rep from * 14 times; [cl in next ch-2 sp, ch 2] 3 times; join with sl st in top of beg cl. *(128 ch-2 sps)*

Rnd 22: Sl st in next ch-2 sp, in same sp work (beg cl, ch 2, cl); ch 2, [cl in next ch-2 sp, ch 2] 7 times; *in next ch-2 sp work (cl, ch2) twice; [cl in next ch-2 sp, ch 2] 7 times; rep from * around; join with sl st in top of beg cl. *(144 ch-2 sps)*

Rnd 23: Sl st in next ch-2 sp, beg cl in same sp, ch 2, [cl in next ch-2 sp, ch 2] twice; in next ch-2 sp work (cl, ch2) twice; *[cl in next ch-2 sp, ch 2] 8 times; in next ch-2 sp work (cl, ch2) twice; rep from * 14 times; [cl in next ch-2 sp, ch 2) 5 times; join with sl st in top of beg cl. *(160 ch-2 sps)*

Edging

Sl st in next ch-2 sp, ch 1, sc in same sp; ch 3, dc in 3rd ch from hook; *sc in next ch-2 sp, ch 3, dc in 3rd ch from hook; rep from * around; join with sl st in first sc. Fasten off and weave in ends. ◆

Shadow Box Trellis

An intriguing trellis pattern worked in treble stitches on both sides gives this buttery-yellow reversible afghan dramatic visual interest.

DESIGN BY DIANE POELLOT

Skill Level

BEGINNER

Size

45 x 65 inches

Materials

- Super bulky (super chunky) weight yarn: 72 oz/1788 yds/2040g butter yellow
- Size K/10½/6.5mm crochet hook or size needed to obtain gauge
- Yarn needle

6 SUPER BULKY

Gauge

2 tr rows = 2½ inches; 8 tr sts = 3½ inches

Check gauge to save time.

Pattern Note

Weave in loose ends as work progresses.

Afghan

Row 1: Ch 101, sc in 2nd ch from hook, sc in each rem ch across, turn. *(100 sc)*

Rows 2–56: Ch 3 *(counts as first dc throughout)*, dc in next st, [sk next 2 sts, tr in each of next 2 sts, working behind tr sts just made, tr in each of the 2 sk sts, sk next 2 sts, tr in each of next 2 sts, working in front of tr sts just made, tr in each of the 2 sk sts] 24 times, dc in each of last 2 sts, turn.

Row 57: Ch 1, sc in each st across, fasten off. ✦

Gossamer Throw

The name says it all in this luxurious, light-as-air throw stitched in a blend of soft plush and mohair-type yarns that make it perfect for cool summer nights.

BY MARGRET WILLSON

Skill Level

■■■▢
INTERMEDIATE

Finished Size
45 x 64 inches

Materials
- TLC Amore medium (worsted) weight yarn (6 oz/278 yds/170g per skein): 3 skeins #3103 vanilla (A)
- Wendy Paris Mohair medium (worsted) weight yarn (1¾ oz/109 yds/50g per ball): 9 balls #1255 horizon (B)
- Size L/11/8mm crochet hook or size needed to obtain gauge
- Yarn needle

Gauge
10 sts = 4 inches; 10 rows = 4 inches

Pattern Notes
Weave in loose ends as work progresses.

Throw is crocheted vertically.

Throw
Row 1: With A, ch 150, sc in 2nd ch from hook, sc in each rem ch across, turn. *(149 sc)*

Row 2: Ch 4 *(counts as first dc, ch-1)*, sk next st, dc in next st, [ch 1, sk next st, dc in next st] across, **change colour** *(see Stitch Guide, p. 31)* to B in last st, turn. *(75 dc; 74 ch-1 sps)*

Row 3: Ch 1, [sc in dc, working behind ch-1 sp, dc in sk st 2 rows below] across, ending with sc in 3rd ch of beg ch-4, turn. *(149 sts)*

Row 4: Ch 3 *(counts as first dc)*, [dc in next dc, ch 1, sk next sc] across, ending with dc in each of last 2 sts, change colour to A, turn.

Row 5: Ch 1, sc in each of first 2 dc, [working behind ch-1 sp, dc in sk st 2 rows below, sc in next dc] across, ending with sc in last st, turn.

Rows 6–105: [Rep rows 2-5 consecutively] 25 times. At the end of row 105, change colour to A.

Row 106: Ch 1, sc in each st across, fasten off.

Fringe
Work Fringe in ends of rows. Cut 5 strands each 20 inches long for each Fringe. Fold strands in half, with WS facing, insert hook into end of dc row of same colour, draw strands through at fold to form a lp on hook, draw cut ends through lp on hook, pull gently to secure. Rep Fringe in each row matching row colour. ✦

Tantalizing Thyme

Cool shades of green give fresh summertime appeal to this lacy, patchwork-style throw.

DESIGN BY JOYCE NORDSTROM

Skill Level

EASY

Finished Size
Approximately 52 x 63 inches

Materials
- TLC Essentials medium (worsted) weight yarn (6 oz/312 yds/170g per skein): 3 skeins each #2672 light thyme (B) and #2673 medium thyme (C), 2 skeins each #2675 dark thyme (D) and #2316 winter white (A)
- Size I/9/5.5mm crochet hook or sized needed to obtain gauge

Gauge
Motif = 5½ inches square
Check gauge to save time.

Special Stitches
Beginning cluster (beg cl):
Keeping last lp of each dc on hook, 2 dc in st or sp indicated, yo and draw through all 3 lps on hook.
Cluster (cl): Ch 3, keeping last lp of each dc on hook, 3 dc in st or sp indicated, yo and draw through all 4 lps on hook.

Pattern Notes
Join with slip stitch unless otherwise noted.

Refer to layout diagram for Motif colour.

First Motif
Rnd 1 (RS): With A, ch 4, join to form a ring, **beg cl** (see Special Stitches) in ring, [ch 3, **cl** (see Special Stitches) in ring] 7 times, ch 1, join with hdc in top of beg cl. (8 cls)
Rnd 2: Beg cl over joining hdc, *ch 3, sc in next ch-3 sp, ch 3, [cl, ch 3, cl] in next ch-3 sp (corner); rep from * twice more, ch 3, sc in next ch-3 sp, ch 3, cl in next sp, ch 1, join with hdc in top of beg cl.
Rnd 3: Beg cl over joining hdc, *[ch 3, sc in next ch-3 sp] twice, ch 3, (cl, ch 3, cl) in corner ch-3 sp; rep from * twice more, [ch 3, sc in next ch-3 sp] twice, ch 3, cl in next sp, ch 1, join with hdc in top of beg cl.
Rnd 4: Beg cl over joining hdc, *[ch 3, sc in next ch-3 sp] 3 times, ch 3, [cl, ch 3, cl] in corner ch-3 sp; rep from * twice more, [ch 3, sc in next ch-3 sp] 3 times, ch 3, cl in next ch-3 sp, ch 1, join with hdc in top of beg cl. Fasten off.

Second Motif
Referring to Assembly Diagram for colour and placement, work same as Rnds 1–3 of First Motif.
Rnd 4 (joining rnd): Beg cl over joining hdc, [ch 3, sc in next ch-3 sp] 3 times, ch 3, [cl, ch 3, cl] in corner ch-3 sp, [ch 3, sc in next ch-3 sp] 3 times, ch 3, cl in corner ch-3 sp, ch 1, sl st in corresponding corner ch-3 sp on adjacent motif; ch 1, cl in same sp on working motif, [ch 1, sl st in corresponding ch-3 sp of adjacent motif, ch 1, sl st in next ch-3 sp on working motif] 3 times, ch 1, sl st in corresponding ch-3 sp on adjacent motif, ch 1, cl in next ch-3 sp on working motif, ch 1, sl st in corresponding corner ch-3 sp on adjacent motif, ch 1, cl in corner ch-3 sp on working motif, [ch 3, sc in next ch-3 sp] 3 times, ch 3, cl in next ch-3 sp, ch 1, join with hdc in top of beg cl. Fasten off.

Remaining Motifs
Referring to Assembly Diagram for colour and placement, work same as Second Motif, joining to adjacent motifs in similar

manner and making sure all
4-corner joinings are secure.

Border

Rnd 1: With RS facing, attach A
in any corner ch-3 sp, beg cl in
same sp, *[ch 3, sc in next ch-3
sp] 4 times, ch 3, sc in motif
joining; rep from * across to last
motif, [ch 3, sc in next ch-3 sp] 4
times, ch 3, (cl, ch 3, cl) in corner
ch-3 sp; rep from * in similar
manner around joining in top of
beg cl. Fasten off.

Rnd 2: Attach B in any corner
ch-3 sp, beg cl in same sp, *[ch 3,
sc in next ch-3 sp] to next corner,
ch 3, (cl, ch 3, cl) in corner ch-3 sp;
rep from * twice more, [ch 3, sc in
next ch-3 sp] to next corner, ch 3,
(cl, ch 3) in same sp as beg cl, sl st
in top of beg cl. Fasten off.

Rnd 3: With C, rep Rnd 2.

Rnd 4: Attach D in any corner
ch-3 sp, beg cl in same sp, *[ch-3,
sc in next ch 3 sp, ch 3, cl in next
ch-3 sp] to corner ch-3 sp, ch 3,
(cl, ch 3, cl) in corner sp; rep from
* twice more, [ch 3, sc in next
ch-3 sp, ch 3, cl in next ch-3 sp] to
beg corner, ch 3, (cl, ch 3) in beg
corner, join in top of beg cl.
Fasten off and weave in all ends. ◆

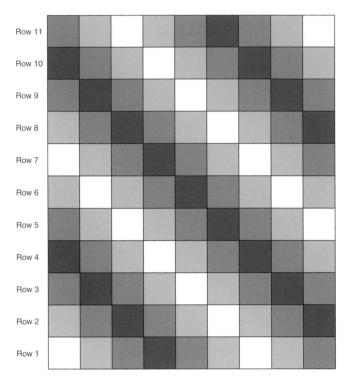

COLOR KEY
☐ Winter White
▨ Light Thyme
▨ Medium Thyme
■ Dark Thyme

Row 11
Row 10
Row 9
Row 8
Row 7
Row 6
Row 5
Row 4
Row 3
Row 2
Row 1

Tantalizing Thyme
Assembly Diagram

Summer Breeze Throw

Puffy white daisies with a hint of shimmer stand out on a pretty pastel background in this gorgeous throw that's as light as a summer breeze.

DESIGN BY DIANE STONE

Skill Level

INTERMEDIATE

Finished Size
48½ x 61½ inches

Materials
- Red Heart Baby Econo medium (worsted) weight yarn (6 oz/480 yds/170g per skein): 2 skeins #1001 white, 1 skein #1224 baby yellow
- Red Heart Super Saver medium (worsted) weight yarn (7 oz/364 yds/198g per skein): 3 skeins #774 light raspberry, 2 skeins #661 frosty green
- Size H/8/5mm crochet hook or size needed to obtain gauge

Gauge
Daisy = 3½ inches in diameter; strip width = 7¾ inches

Pattern Notes
Weave in loose ends as work progresses.

Join rounds with a slip stitch unless otherwise stated. Centre of Daisy will cup and this produces the necessary puffiness.

Special Stitches
Shell: (3 dc, ch 2, 3 dc) in indicated st.

Beginning shell (beg shell): Ch 3, (2 dc, ch 2, 3 dc) in same st as beg ch-3.

Daisy
Make 72.
Centre
Rnd 1: With baby yellow, leaving a slight length at beg, ch 2, 8 sc in 2nd ch from hook, join in beg sc, pull rem beg end to close opening. *(8 sc)*

Rnds 2 & 3: Ch 1, sc in each sc around, join in beg sc. At the end of rnd 3, fasten off. *(8 sc)*

Petals
Rnd 4: Attach white in any sc of rnd 3, ch 4 *(counts as first tr)*, (3 tr, ch 3, 4 tr) in same sc as beg ch-4, ch 3, [4 tr, ch 3] twice in each rem sc around, join in 4th ch of beg ch-4, fasten off. *(16 tr Petals)*

Leaf Trim
Make 6 strips of 12 daisies in each row.
First Daisy
Attach frosty green in any ch-3

sp of rnd 4 of Petals, ch 1, sc in same ch-3 sp, ch 5, *sc in next ch-3 sp, ch 1, sc in next ch-3 sp, ch 5, sc in next ch-3 sp, ch 5, sl st in 2nd ch from hook, hdc in next ch, dc in each of next 2 chs**, sc in next ch-3 sp, ch 5, rep from * around, ending last rep at **, join in beg sc, fasten off.

Second Daisy
Attach frosty green in any ch-3 sp of rnd 4 of Petals, ch 1, sc in same ch-3 sp, ch 5, *sc in next ch-3 sp, ch 1, sc in next ch-3 sp, ch 5, sc in next ch-3 sp, ch 5, with WS facing, sl st in tip of leaf on previous Daisy, sl st in 2nd ch from hook, hdc in next ch, dc in each of next 2 chs, sc in next ch-3 sp of working Daisy, ch 2, sc in next ch-5 sp on previous Daisy, ch 2, sc in next ch-3 sp on working Daisy, ch 1, sc in next ch-3 sp on working Daisy, ch 2, sc in next ch-5 sp on previous Daisy, ch 2, sc in next ch-3 sp on working Daisy, ch 5, sl st in tip of next leaf on previous Daisy, *sl st in 2nd ch from hook, hdc in next ch, dc in each of last 2 chs**, sc in next ch-3 sp on working Daisy,

ch 5, sc in next ch-3 sp, ch 1, sc in next ch-3 sp, ch 5, sc in next ch-3 sp, ch 5, rep from * around, ending last rep at ** join in beg sc, fasten off.

Join rem 10 daisies in same manner as 2nd Daisy.

Edging
First Strip
Rnd 1: Attach light raspberry with sl st in first ch-5 sp to the left of corner leaf in right upper corner and working across long edge, **beg shell** (see Special Stitches, p. 135) in same ch-5 sp, **shell** (see Special Stitches) in next ch-5 sp, ch 7, [shell in each of next 2 ch-5 sps, ch 7] around, join in 3rd ch of beg ch-3.

Rnd 2: Sl st into ch-2 sp of beg shell, beg shell in same ch-2 sp, shell in ch-2 sp of next shell, *ch 1, working over ch-7 of previous row and between leaves, work 2 dc, ch 1, [shell in next shell, ch 1] twice, rep from * around, working at each of the 4 corner leaves, ch 1, working into 4th ch of ch-7 and tip of corner leaf, shell in tip of leaf, ch 1, ending with join in 3rd ch of beg ch-3, fasten off.

Second Strip
Rnd 1: Rep rnd 1 of First Strip.
Rnd 2: Sl st into ch-2 sp of shell, ch 3, 2 dc in same ch sp, ch 1, holding previous strip next to working strip, sl st in ch-2 sp of adjacent shell, ch 1, 3 dc in same ch-2 sp as beg ch-3, ch 1, 3 dc in ch-2 sp of next shell, ch 1, sl st in adjacent ch-2 sp on previous strip, ch 1, 3 dc in same ch-2 sp on working strip, *ch 1, working over ch-7 sp and into sp between leaves, work 2 dc, [ch 1, 3 dc in ch-2 sp of next shell, ch 1, sl st in adjacent ch-2 sp on previous strip, ch 1, 3 dc in same ch-2 sp of shell on working strip] twice, rep from * across edge, ch 1, working over ch-7 of previous row and between leaves, work 2 dc, ch 1, [shell in next shell, ch 1] twice, rep from * around, working at each of the 4 corner leaves, ch 1, working into 4th ch of ch-7 and tip of corner leaf, shell in tip of leaf, ending with join in 3rd ch of beg ch-3, fasten off.

Join rem strips in the same manner as 2nd Strip was joined to First Strip joining adjacent side in last rnd.

Edging
Rnd 1: Working across top of throw, attach light raspberry in upper right corner ch-2 of shell (ch-2 sp of shell to left above corner leaf), beg shell in same ch-2 sp, *[(ch 1, sc, ch 1) in sp between shells, shell in next shell] 3 times, ch 1, sc in next ch-1 sp, sl st in each of next 3 dc of shell, sc in ch-2 sp of shell, ch 3, sc in ch-2 sp of next shell on next strip, sl st in each of next 3 dc of shell, sc in next ch-1 sp, ch 1, shell in ch-2 sp of next shell, rep from * 4 times, [ch 1, sc in next ch-1 sp between shells, ch 1, shell in next shell] 5 times, [ch 1, sc in next ch-1 sp, ch 3, sk next 2 dc, sc in next ch-1 sp, shell in ch-2 sp of next shell, (ch 1, sc, ch 1) in next ch-1 sp between shells, shell in next shell] 11 times, (ch 1, sc, ch 1) in next ch-1 sp between shells, shell in next shell, rep from * around, join in top of beg ch-3.

Rnd 2: Sl st into corner ch-2 sp of shell, ch 4 (counts as first dc, ch 1), ({dc, ch 1} 4 times, dc) in corner ch-2 sp above a corner leaf, *[ch 1, sc in next ch-1 sp, sk next sc, sc in next ch-1 sp, (ch 1, dc) 6 times in ch-2 sp of next shell] 3 times, ch 1, sc in next ch-1 sp, ch 1, 2 dc in next ch-3 sp, ch 1, sc in next ch-1 sp, (ch 1, dc) 6 times in ch-2 sp of next shell, rep from * 4 times, [ch 1, sc in next ch-1 sp, sk next sc, sc in next ch-1 sp, (ch 1, dc) 6 times in ch-2 sp of next shell] 5 times, [ch 1, 2 dc in next ch-3 sp, (ch 1, dc) 6 times in ch-2 sp of next shell, ch 1, sc in next ch-1 sp, sk next sc, sc in next ch-1 sp, (ch 1, dc) 6 times in ch-2 sp of next shell] 11 times, ch 1, sc in next ch-1 sp, sk next sc, sc in next ch-1 sp**, (ch 1, dc) 6 times in corner ch-2 sp above a corner leaf, rep from * around, ending last rep at **, join in 3rd ch of beg ch-4, fasten off. ◆

Spellbinding

A variety of yarns with an enticing array of textures makes this delectable design a sensory delight!

DESIGN BY MARTY MILLER

Skill Level

EASY

Finished Size
Approximately 45 x 55 inches, excluding fringe

Materials
- Bernat Baby Bubbles bulky (chunky) weight yarn (2½ oz/105 yds/70g per ball): 4 balls #75315 pretty bubbles (A)
- Patons Be Mine bulky (chunky) weight yarn (1¾ oz/95 yds/50g per ball): 4 balls #63215 sweetie aqua (B)
- Lion Brand Homespun bulky (chunky) weight yarn (6 oz/185 yds/170g per skein): 2 skeins #300 hepplewhite (D), 2 skeins #379 cobalt (E)
- Patons Brilliant light (light worsted) weight yarn (1¾ oz/175 yds/50g per ball): 3 balls #03416 perfect pastels (C)
- Lion Brand Romance super bulky (super chunky) weight yarn (8 oz/ 480 yds/224g per ball): 1 ball #143 lavender (F)

- Wendy Paris Mohair medium (worsted) weight yarn (1¾ oz/109 yds/50g per ball): 3 balls #1211 lake (G)
- Size N/15/10mm crochet hook or size needed obtain gauge
- Tapestry needle

Gauge
9 dc = 5 inches

Special Stitch
Front post double crochet (fpdc): Yo, insert hook from front to back to front around **post** (see Stitch Guide, p. 31) of st indicated, draw lp through, [yo, draw through 2 lps on hook] twice.

Afghan
Note: Afghan is worked lengthwise.

Row 1 (RS): With D, leaving 12-inch end, loosely ch 102; dc in 4th ch from hook (beg 3 sk chs count as a dc) and in each rem ch. (100 dc) Fasten off, leaving 12-inch end. Leaving 12-inch end, join F in sp between last 2 dc, turn.

Row 2: Ch 2, sk first st, **fpdc** (see Special Stitch) around each of next 98 dc, hdc in sp between last dc and beg 3 sk chs. Fasten off, leaving 12-inch end. Leaving 12-inch end, join B in sp between last 2 fpdc of row, turn.

Row 3: Ch 2, sk first st, fpdc around each of next 98 dc, hdc in sp between last dc and beg ch-2. Fasten off, leaving 12-inch end. Leaving 12-inch end, join E in sp between last 2 fpdc of row, turn.

Rows 4–66: Rep row 3 using following colour sequence: E, A, G, C, D, F, B.

Rows 67–71: Rep row 3 using following colour sequence: E, A, G, C, D. At end of row 71, do not join new colour.

Fringe
Following Fringe instructions on page 172, make Single Knot Fringe. Cut 24-inch strands of yarn. Use 1 strand for each knot of fringe. Matching colour of yarn with colour of row, tie 2 knots in end of each row, including 12-inch end in 1 of the knots. Tie knots across each short end of afghan. ✦

For the Man

Your favourite guy will enjoy the cozy warmth and masculine look of this plush, earthy throw.

DESIGN BY MARTY MILLER

Skill Level

EASY

Finished Size
Approximately 44 x 55 inches

Materials
- Lion Brand Homespun bulky (chunky) weight yarn (6 oz/185 yds/170g per skein): 10 skeins #395 meadow
- Size N/15/10mm crochet hook or size needed to obtain gauge
- Tapestry needle

Gauge
8 fpdc = 4 inches

Special Stitch
Front post double crochet (fpdc): Yo, insert hook from front to back to front around **post** (see Stitch Guide, p. 31) of st indicated, draw lp through, [yo, draw through 2 lps on hook] twice.

Block
Make 20.
Row 1 (WS): Loosely ch 24; dc in 4th ch from hook (beg 3 sk chs count as a dc) and in each rem ch, turn. (22 dc)
Row 2 (RS): Ch 2 (counts as a hdc on this and following rows),

sk first dc, **fpdc** (see Special Stitch) around each of next 20 dc; hdc in sp between last 2 dc, turn.
Row 3: Ch 2, sk first hdc, fpdc around each of next 20 fpdc; hdc in sp between last st and beg ch-2, turn.
Rows 4–22: Rep row 3. Fasten off and weave in ends.

Assembly
Referring to diagram on page 135, arrange Blocks in 5 rows of 4 Blocks each. For each Block A, place last row at top; for each Block B, place last row at left-hand edge. To join Blocks, hold 2 Blocks with WS tog. Working through both thicknesses at same time, join yarn in upper right-hand corner; ch 1, sc in same sp; sc evenly spaced across side. Fasten off and weave in ends. Join rem Blocks in rows; then join rows in similar

manner, making sure all 4-corner junctions are secure.

Border
Rnd 1 (RS): Hold piece with RS facing you and 1 short end at top; join yarn in upper right-hand corner; ch 1, 3 sc in same corner; sc evenly spaced around edge, working 3 sc in each rem corner, sc in each dc and 1 or 2 sc in each row end, keeping rnd flat; join with sl st in first sc.
Rnd 2: Ch 1, sc in same sc as joining; 3 sc in next sc; *sc in each sc to 2nd sc of next corner; 3 sc in 2nd sc; rep from * twice; sc in each sc to first sc; join with sl st in first sc. Fasten off and weave in ends. ✦

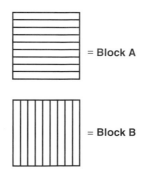

= Block A

= Block B

Block A	Block B	Block A	Block B
Block B	Block A	Block B	Block A
Block A	Block B	Block A	Block B
Block B	Block A	Block B	Block A
Block A	Block B	Block A	Block B

Assembly Diagram

Fallen Petals

Rows of alternating triple crochet shells create the effect of plush petals in this luscious, lacy throw.

DESIGN BY LISA THOMM

Skill Level

EASY

Size

48 x 66 inches

Materials

- TLC Essentials medium (worsted) weight yarn (6 oz/312 yds/170g per skein): 8 skeins #2531 light plum
- Size L/11/8mm crochet hook or size needed to obtain gauge
- Yarn needle

Gauge

Pattern rep of rows 2–5 = 3 inches; 1 shell, 1 sc and 2 ch-2 sps = 3½ inches
Check gauge to save time.

Pattern Notes

Weave in loose ends as work progresses.

Join rounds with a slip stitch unless otherwise stated.

Hold two strands of yarn together throughout afghan.

Special Stitch

Shell: 4 tr in indicated st.

Afghan

Row 1 (RS): Ch 98, sc in 2nd ch from hook, [ch 2, sk next 3 chs, **shell** (see Special Stitch) in next ch, ch 2, sk next

3 chs, sc in next ch] across, turn. (12 shells; 13 sc; 24 ch-2 sps)

Row 2: Ch 1, sc in first sc, [ch 3, sk next tr, sc in next tr, ch 3, sk next 2 tr, sc in next sc] across, turn. (25 sc; 24 ch-3 sps)

Row 3: Ch 4 (counts as first tr throughout), tr in same st, ch 2, sc in next sc, ch 2, [shell in next sc, ch 2, sc in next sc, ch 2] across to last sc, 2 tr in last sc, turn. (11 shells; 12 sc; 24 ch-2 sps; 2 half shells)

Row 4: Ch 1, sc in same st, ch 3, sk next tr, sc in next sc, ch 3, sk next tr, [sc in next tr, ch 3, sk next 2 tr, sc in next sc, ch 3, sk next tr] across to ch-4, sc in top of ch-4, turn.

Row 5: Ch 1, sc in first sc, [ch 2, shell in next sc, ch 2, sc in next sc] across, turn. (12 shells; 13 sc; 24 ch-2 sps)

Rows 6–73: [Rep rows 2-5 consecutively] 17 times.

Row 74: Rep row 2, ch 1, sl st in end of row, **do not fasten off**, turn.

Border

Rnd 1 (RS): Ch 1, 3 sc in end of first row for corner, [4 sc in next ch-3 sp, 3 sc in next ch-3 sp] across (84 sc), 3 sc in end of row for corner, working in ends of rows, sc in end of each sc row and 3 sc in end of tr row across (109 sc), 3 sc in next st for corner,

working across opposite side of foundation ch, [4 sc in next ch sp, 3 sc in next ch sp] across (84 sc), 3 sc in end st for corner, working in ends of rows, sc in end of each sc row and 3 sc in end of tr row across (109 sc), join in beg sc. (398 sc total)

Rnd 2: Ch 1, sc in first st, *[ch 5, sc in next st] twice, ch 5, sk next 4 sts, [sc in next st, ch 5, sk next 4 sts] across to next 3-sc corner, sc in next sc, [ch 5, sc in next sc] twice, ch 5, sk next 4 sc, [sc in next sc, ch 5, sk next 4 sc] across to next 3-sc corner, rep from * around, join in beg sc. (2 ch-5 lps each corner; 17 ch-5 lps each top and bottom; 22 each side; total 86 ch-5 lps)

Rnd 3: Sl st in next 3 chs, ch 1, (sc, ch 3, sc) in same ch, ch 5, [(sc, ch 3, sc) in 3rd ch of next ch-5 sp, ch 5] around, join in beg sc.

Rnds 4–6: Sl st in each of next 3 chs, sl st in next sc, sl st in each of next 3 chs, ch 1, (sc, ch 3, sc) in same ch, ch 5, [(sc, ch 3, sc) in 3rd ch of next ch-5 sp, ch 5] around, join in beg sc.

Rnd 7: Sl st in next ch-3 sp, ch 1, sc in same ch sp, [ch 3, sc] twice in same ch sp, ch 2, sc in 3rd ch of next ch-5 sp, ch 2, *sc in next ch-3 sp, [ch 3, sc] twice in same ch-3 sp, ch 2, sc in 3rd ch of ch-5 sp, ch 2, rep from * around, join in beg sc, fasten off. ◆

Lumberjack Throw

The masculine feel of bold red and black stripes in this reversible throw evokes thoughts of the rugged woodsmen of the Pacific Northwest.

DESIGN BY KATHLEEN GAREN

Skill Level

EASY

Size
46 x 56 inches

Materials
- Red Heart Super Saver medium (worsted) weight yarn (7 oz/364 yds/198g): 3 skeins #312 black, 2 skeins #390 hot red
- Size K/10½/6.5mm crochet hook or size needed to obtain gauge
- Yarn needle

Gauge
5 sts = 2 inches; 4 rows = 2 inches
Check gauge to save time.

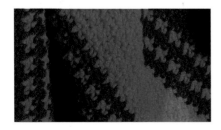

Pattern Notes
Weave in loose ends as work progresses.

Join rounds with a slip stitch unless otherwise stated.

Afghan
Row 1: With black, ch 141 loosely, sc in 2nd ch from hook, sc in each rem ch across, turn. *(140 sc)*

Row 2: Ch 1, sc in first st, sc in next st, [sc in next st, dc in next st] across, turn.

Row 3: Ch 1, [sc in dc, dc in sc] across, turn.

Rows 4–7: Rep row 3. At the end of row 7, fasten off, turn.

Row 8: With red, rep row 3, fasten off.

Row 9: With black, rep row 3, fasten off.

Rows 10 & 11: Rep rows 8 and 9.

Rows 12–18: With red, rep row 3. At the end of row 18, fasten off.

Row 19: With black, rep row 3, fasten off.

Row 20: With red, rep row 3, fasten off.

Rows 21 & 22: Rep rows 19 and 20.

Rows 23–31: With black, rep row 3. At the end of row 31, fasten off.

Rows 32–35: Rep rows 8–11.

Rows 36–83: [Rep rows 12-23 consecutively] twice.

Rows 84–94: Rep rows 12–22.

Rows 95–100: With black, rep row 3.

Row 101: With black, ch 1, sc in each st across, do not fasten off.

Border
Rnd 102: Ch 3 *(counts as first dc)*, dc in same sp as last sc, sk 2 rows, [sc in next st, ch 3, dc in same st, sk next 2 sts or next 2 rows, sc in next st] around outer edge, join in 3rd ch of beg ch-3, fasten off. ✦

Mountain Forests

A deep ripple design in shades of cool forest green brings to mind a lushly wooded mountainside in this beautiful afghan that works up quickly with double-stranded yarn and a large hook.

DESIGN BY CHRISTINE GRAZIOSO MOODY

Skill Level
◼◼◻◻
EASY

Size
48 x 64 inches

Materials
- Red Heart Super Saver medium (worsted) weight yarn (7 oz/364 yds/198g): 11 oz #312 black (A), 9 oz each #633 dark sage (B),
- Bernat Super Value medium (worsted) weight yarn (7 oz/382 yds/197g per skein): 9 oz #07742 medium sea green (C), #631 light sage (D), #661 frosty green (E) and #313 aran (F)
- Size N/15/10mm crochet hook or size needed to obtain gauge
- Yarn needle

Gauge
With 2 strands of yarn held tog, 4 sts = 2 inches; 2 dc rows = 2½ inches

Pattern Notes
Weave in loose ends as work progresses.

Join rounds with a slip stitch unless otherwise stated.

Work with 2 strands of same colour yarn held together throughout.

Special Stitch
Front post treble crochet (fptr): Yo over hook twice, insert hook from front to back to front again around the vertical post of indicated st on row before last, yo, draw up a lp, [yo, draw through 2 lps on hook] 3 times, sk st directly behind fptr on working row.

Afghan
Row 1: With A, ch 115, **dc dec** (see Stitch Guide, p. 31) in 4th and 5th chs from hook, dc in each of next 5 chs, (2 dc, ch 1, 2 dc) in next ch, dc in each of next 5 chs, *dc dec in next 5 chs, dc in each of next 5 chs, (2 dc, ch 1, 2 dc) in next ch, dc in each of next 5 chs, rep from * across, ending with dc dec in last 3 chs, turn. (106 sts; 7 ch sps)

Row 2: Ch 3 (beg ch-3 is not used or counted as a st), dc dec in next 2 sts, dc in each of next 5 sts, (2 dc, ch 1, 2 dc) in next ch sp, dc in each of next 5 sts, *dc dec in next 5 sts, dc in each of next 5 sts, (2 dc, ch 1, 2 dc) in next ch sp, dc in each of next 5 sts, rep from * across to last 3 sts, dc dec in next 3 sts, turn, fasten off.

Row 3: Attach B with sl st in first st, ch 3, dc dec in next 2 sts, *[dc in each of next 3 sts, **fptr** (see Special Stitch) around last st before next ch sp on row before last, dc in next st on last row, (2 dc, ch 1, 2 dc) in next ch sp, dc in next st, fptr around first st after ch sp on row before last, dc in each of next 3 sts on last row], dc dec in next 5 sts, rep from * 5 more times, rep between [ ], dc dec in next 3 sts, turn.

Rows 4–50: [Rep rows 2 and 3 alternately] 24 times, working in colour sequence of C, D, E, F, A and B, ending with row 2 and A. ◆

Cascades

A soft, subtle ripple design highlighted in cream against a background of deep blue creates the impression of a gently cascading waterfall in this cozy throw.

DESIGN BY CHRISTINE GRAZIOSO MOODY

Skill Level

■■□□

EASY

Finished Size

46 x 62 inches

Materials

- Red Heart Light & Lofty super bulky (super chunky) weight yarn (6 oz/140 yds/170g per skein): 6 skeins #9380 antique blue, 1 skein #9334 café au lait
- Size P/16/11.5mm crochet hook or size needed to obtain gauge
- Yarn needle

Gauge

4 dc = 2¾ inches

Pattern Notes

Weave in loose ends as work progresses.

Join rounds with a slip stitch unless otherwise stated.

Throw

Row 1 (RS): With antique blue, ch 85, dc in 4th ch from hook, dc in each of next 3 chs, sk next 2 chs, dc in each of next 3 chs, [(dc, ch 2, dc) in next ch, dc in each of next 3 chs, sk next 2 chs, dc in each of next 3 chs] 8 times, 2 dc in last ch, turn.

Row 2 (WS): Ch 3 *(counts as first dc)*, working in **front lps** *(see Stitch Guide, p. 31)* only, dc in same st as beg ch-3, dc in each of next 3 sts, sk next 2 sts, dc in each of next 3 sts, [dc in first ch of ch-2 sp, ch 2, dc in 2nd ch of ch-2 sp, dc in each of next 3 sts, sk next 2 sts, dc in each of next 3 sts] 8 times, 2 dc in last st, draw up a lp, remove hook and drop yarn, **do not fasten off**.

Row 3 (RS): Working in rem free **back lps** *(see Stitch Guide)* of each st, attach café au lait with sl st in first st, ch 1, sc in same st, sc in each st and each ch across, fasten off, **do not turn**.

Note: *When working row 4, sk sc sts of previous row unless otherwise indicated to work in specific sts.*

Row 4 (RS): Pick up dropped lp of antique blue, ch 3, dc in first sc of previous row, dc in each of next 3 dc, [dc in sc worked in first ch, ch 2, dc in sc worked in 2nd ch, dc in each of next 3 dc, sk next 2 dc, dc in each of next 3 dc] across, ending with dc in last sc of previous row, dc in last dc, turn.

Rows 5 & 6: Ch 3, dc in same st as beg ch-3, dc in each of next 3 dc, sk each of next 2 dc, dc in each of next 3 dc, [(dc, ch 2, dc) in next ch-2 sp, dc in each of next 3 dc, sk each of next 2 dc, dc in each of next 3 dc] across, 2 dc in last dc, turn.

Rows 7–46: [Rep rows 2-6 consecutively] 8 times.

Rows 47–49: Rep rows 2–4. At the end of row 49, fasten off. ◆

North Woods Throw

This cozy, earthy throw, stitched in luxurious bulky yarns, features the subtle, serene woodland colours that perfectly complement a rustic decor.

DESIGN BY KATHERINE ENG

Skill Level

INTERMEDIATE

Finished Size

41 x 57 inches

Materials

- Lion Brand Homespun bulky (chunky) weight yarn (6 oz/185 yds/170g per skein): 3 skeins #309 deco, 2 skeins #326 ranch
- Lion Brand Chenille Thick and Quick bulky (super chunky) weight yarn (100 yds per skein): 2 skeins each #178 basil and #155 champagne
- Lion Brand Wool-Ease medium (worsted) weight yarn (3 oz/197 yds/85g per skein): 2 skeins each #099 fisherman and #127 mink
- Plymouth Galway medium (worsted) weight yarn (3½ oz/210 yds/100g per ball): 2 balls #138 camel
- Sizes F/5/3.75mm, G/6/4mm and H/8/5mm crochet hooks or size needed to obtain gauge

Gauge

Size F hook: rnds 1 and 2 = 3 inches; completed square = 5¾ inches

Pattern Notes

Weave in loose ends as work progresses.

Join rounds with a slip stitch unless otherwise stated.

When joining motifs, alternate Motifs A and B throughout.

Special Stitches

Popcorn (pc): 3 dc in indicated st, drop lp from hook, insert hook front to back through top of first dc, pick up dropped lp, draw lp through st on hook.

Shell: 3 dc in indicated st.

Motifs A [B]
Make 32 [31].

Rnd 1: With size F hook and fisherman, ch 4, join in first ch to form a ring, ch 3 *(counts as first dc)* [pc *(see Special Stitches)* in ring, ch 3] 8 times, join in top of first pc, fasten off. *(8 pc, 8 ch-3 sps)*

Rnd 2: With size G hook, draw up lp of camel in any ch-3 sp, ch 1, (2 sc, ch 2, 2 sc) in same sp, *(3 dc, ch 2, 3 dc) in next ch-3 sp**, (2 sc, ch 2, 2 sc) in next ch-3 sp, rep from * around, ending last rep at **, join in beg sc, fasten off.

Rnd 3: With size G hook, draw up lp of mink in any corner ch-2 sp, ch 1, sc in same sp, *ch 1, (3 dc, ch 2, 3 dc) in next ch-2 sp, ch 1**, sc in next ch-2 sp, rep from * around, ending last rep at **, join in beg sc, fasten off.

Rnd 4: With size H hook, draw up a lp of basil [champagne] in any st, ch 1, sc in each st and in each ch-1 sp around working (sc, ch 2, sc) in each corner ch-2 sp, join in beg sc, fasten off. *(44 sc, 4 ch-2 sps)*

Note: *Work rnd 5 around first square of Motif A, then join motifs as specified on rnd 5 of remaining motifs as work progresses.*

Rnd 5: With size H hook, draw up a lp of ranch [deco] in 2nd sc to the left of any corner ch-2 sp, ch 1, (sc, ch 2, sc) in same sc, [sk 1 sc, (sc, ch 2, sc) in next sc] around, working at each corner (sc, ch 4, sc) in corner ch-2 sps, join in beg sc, fasten off. *(20 ch-2 sps, 4 ch-4 sps)*

Joining motifs: Alternating Motifs A and B and working rnd 5, join in 7 rows of 9 motifs. To join corner sps where 2 corners meet, continuing in pattern st, ch 2, drop lp, draw lp under to over through opposite ch-4 sp, ch 2 and continue. To join ch-2 sps, ch 1, drop lp, draw lp under to over through opposite ch-2 sp, ch 1 and continue. To join where 4 corners meet, ch 2, drop lp, draw lp under to over through opposite ch-4 sp, ch 1, drop lp, sk next ch-4 sp, draw lp under to over through next ch-4 sp, ch 2 and continue.

Border

Rnd 1 (RS): With size H hook, draw up a lp of deco in first ch-2 sp to the left of any corner ch-4 sp, ch 1, sc in same sp, *ch 2, sc in next ch-2 sp *(or ch-4 sp of corners at joining seams)*, rep from * around, working ch 2, (sc, ch 4, sc) in each corner ch-4 sp, join last ch 2 to beg sc, sl st into next ch-2 sp.

Rnd 2: Ch 1, (sc, ch 2, sc) in each ch-2 sp, ({sc, ch 2} 3 times, sc) in each corner ch-4 sp, join in beg sc, fasten off.

Rnd 3: Draw up a lp of camel in any ch-2 sp, ch 1, (sc, ch 2, sc) in each ch-2 sp around, join in beg sc, fasten off, turn.

Rnd 4: Draw up a lp of champagne in any ch-2 sp *(not in a corner)*, ch 1, sc in same sp, [ch 1, sc in next ch-2 sp] around, working at each corner, ch 1, (sc, ch 3, sc) in each corner ch-2 sp, join in beg sc, fasten off, turn.

Rnd 5: Draw up a lp of mink in any sc, ch 1, (sc, ch 2, sc) in each sc and (sc, ch 3, sc) in each corner ch-3 sp, join in beg sc, fasten off, turn.

Rnd 6: Draw up a lp of basil in any sc, rep rnd 4.

Rnd 7: Draw up a lp of ranch in first ch sp to the left of any corner ch-3 sp, ch 1, sc in same sp, [**shell** *(see Special Stitches, p. 151)* in next ch sp, sc in next ch sp] around, working 5 dc in each corner ch-3 sp, join in beg sc.

Rnd 8: With size G hook, *ch 2, (sc, ch 2, sc) in centre dc of next shell, ch 2, sl st in next sc, rep from * around, working at each corner, ch 2, sk 1 dc, (sc, ch 2, sc) in next dc, (sc, ch 3, sc) in next dc, (sc, ch 2, sc) in next dc, ch 2, sk last dc, sl st in next sc, ending with sl st in same st as beg ch-2, fasten off. ✦

Bold Blocks Afghan

Continued from page 38

Rows 73–81: Rep row 2. At the end of row 81, change colour to soft taupe, turn.

Rows 82–90: Rep row 2. At the end of row 90, change colour to richest red, turn.

Rows 91–99: Rep row 2. At the end of row 99, change colour to soft taupe, turn.

Rows 100–108: Rep row 2. At the end of row 108, change colour to black, turn.

Rows 109–117: Rep row 2. At the end of row 117, change colour to natural, turn.

Rows 118–126: Rep row 2. At the end of row 126, change colour to richest red, turn.

Rows 127–135: Rep row 2. At the end of row 135, change colour to natural, turn.

Rows 136–144: Rep row 2. At the end of row 144, change colour to black, turn.

Rows 145–153: Rep row 2. At the end of row 153, fasten off.

Assembly
Sew the 17 Panels tog, beg with A [B, C, B, A] 4 times. ◆

Bouclé Afghan

Continued from page 44

next ch-2 sp, sc in next sc] across, ending with (sc, ch 3, sc) in last sc, working across first half of bottom, sk next sc, V-st in next ch-3 sp, [sk next sc, sc in next sc, V-st in next ch-3 sp] across, ending with sk next 2 sc**, sc in foundation ch at centre bottom, rep from * around, ending last rep at **, join in beg sc, fasten off.

Rnd 2 (RS): Draw up a lp of A in any ch-3 sp, ch 1, sc in same ch-3 sp, shell in next sc, [sc in each ch-3 sp, shell in next sc] around, join in beg sc.

Rnd 3 (RS): Ch 1, sc in first sc, *ch 2, (sc, ch 2, sc) in next ch-2 sp, ch 2**, sc in next sc, rep from * around, ending last rep at **, join in beg sc, fasten off. ◆

Smoke & Mirrors Afghan

Continued from page 66

Row 14: Rep row 4. Fasten off. **Do not turn.**

Row 15: With RS facing, join B with a sl st in top of ch-3, rep row 2, ending with sc in last inv V-st, sc in last dc. Fasten off. Turn.

Row 16: Working in front lps only, rep row 4.

Row 17: With B, rep row 2.

Row 18: Working in front lps only, rep row 4.

Rows 19–48: Rep rows 2–18 once, then rep rows 2–14. Fasten off at end of row 48.

Finishing
Fringe
Fringe is worked across both short edges.
Cut 4 14-inch strands of A for each row worked in A; cut 2 14-inch strands of B and 2 14-inch strands of C for each pair of rows worked in B and C. Holding 4 strands of A tog, fold in half. With RS facing, insert hook from WS to RS over end st of any A row, *pick up folded end of 4-strand group and draw through to WS to form lp, pull free ends through lp and tighten*. Holding 2 strands B and 2 strands C tog, fold in half. With RS facing, insert hook from WS to RS over end of afghan at centre of any pair of B and C rows, rep from * to *. Continue across first short edge. Rep on rem short edge. Trim ends even. ◆

Wrap-Sody in Blue Blanket Coat
Continued from page 74

Row 53 [57, 65, 75, 83]: Ch 2, dc in each st across with dc dec in last 2 sts, turn. *(127 dc)*

Rows 54–61 [58–65, 66–73, 76–83, 84–91]: [Rep last 2 rows alternately] 4 times. *(119 dc at end of last row)*

Row 62 [66, 74, 84, 92]: Rep row 52 [56, 64, 74, 82]. *(118 dc)*

Row 63 [67, 75, 85, 93]: Ch 2, dc in each st across, turn. Fasten off.

Sleeve

Rnd 1: With RS facing, join with sl st in first dc after bottom of armhole, ch 2, dc in each of next 21 sts, dc dec in next st already worked in, around post of dc at top of armhole and in top of same dc just worked around, dc in each of next 22 chs, dc dec at bottom of armhole in same way as at top, join with sl st in 2nd ch of beg ch-2. *(46 dc)*

Rnds 2–8: [2–8, 2–8, 2–10, 2–10]: Ch 2, dc in each st around, join with sl st in 2nd ch of beg ch-2.

Rnd 9 [9, 9, 11, 11]: Ch 2, dc dec in next 2 sts, dc in each st around to last 3 sts, dc dec in next 2 sts, dc in last st, join with sl st in 2nd ch of beg ch-2. *(44 dc)*

Rnd 10 [10, 10, 12, 12]: Ch 2, dc in each st around, join with sl st in 2nd ch of beg ch-2.

Next rnds: [Rep last 2 rnds alternately] 2 [2, 1, 0, 0] time(s).

Next rnds: Work even until you have 21 rnds total. At end of last rnd, fasten off.

Rep on rem armhole. ◆

Lullaby Luvie
Continued from page 107

Border

Rnd 1: Attach white in last sc made on last row, ch 1, sc in same st as beg ch-1, ch 3, working along side edge, sc in sp formed by the ch sts at end of next row, [ch 3, sk sc at the end of next row, sc in sp formed by ch sts at end of next row] across to corner, ch 3, sc through sc on end of row 1, [ch 3, sc in next sp formed by beg ch] across to next corner, ch 3, sc through first sc on row 1, ch 3, working on side edge, sc in sp formed by the ch st at end of 2nd row, [ch 3, sk sc at end of next row, sc in sp formed by ch sts at end of next row] across to next corner, ch 3, sc in first sc on last row, [ch 3, sc in next ch-3 sp] across, ch 3, join in beg sc. *(216 ch-3 sps)*

Rnd 2: Sl st into first ch-3 sp, ch 1, sc in same sp, ch 3, [sc in next ch-3 sp, ch 3] around, join in beg sc, fasten off. ◆

Posies for Baby
Continued from page 114

7 sc made, draw lp though; in ring work (hdc, dc, hdc)—*petal made;* in ring work (sl st, hdc, dc, hdc)—*petal made;* join with sl st in first sl st in ring—*flower made;* sc in next 6 sc of previous row; *ch 4, join to form ring; turn ring only; in ring work [sl st, hdc, dc, hdc] 3 times—*3 petals made;* insert hook in ring and in 2nd sc of previous 6 sc made, draw lp though; in ring work (hdc, dc, hdc)—*petal made;* in ring work (sl st, hdc, dc, hdc)—*petal made;* join with sl st in first sl st in ring—*flower made;* sc in next 6 sc of previous row; rep from * 5 times, turn.

Note: Change to N hook and pick up A; fasten off B.

Row 11: Rep row 6.

Rows 12–51: [Work rows 2–11 consecutively] 4 times.

Rows 52–59: Rep rows 2–9. Fasten off and weave in all ends. ◆

INDEX

Decorator Throws

Modern Day Warmth Sofa Afghan, 32

Warm Weavings, 34

Watermelon Print Throw, 36

Bold Blocks Afghan, 38

Midnight Magic Throw, 40

Woodland Throw, 43

Bouclé Afghan, 44

Spirals to Surround You, 46

Sun-Washed Tiles, 49

Patchwork Quilt Afghan, 52

Squiggles & Giggles, 55

Puffy Flowers Throw, 59

Gramma & Grandbabies, 60

Warming Trend Versatile Afghan, 64

Smoke & Mirrors Afghan, 66

INDEX

INDEX

INDEX

Our website is stuffed with all kinds of great information

www.companyscoming.com

Save up to 75% on cookbooks

Free recipes and cooking tips

Free newsletter with exclusive o...

Preview new titles

Find older titles no longer in stores